THE
FREE TRADE
DEBATE

THE FREE TRADE DEBATE

Reports of the
Twentieth Century Fund Task Force
on the Future of
American Trade Policy

Background Paper
by Gary Clyde Hufbauer

P
P Priority Press Publications/New York/1989

Library of Congress Cataloging-in-Publication Data

Twentieth Century Fund. Task Force on the Future of American Trade Policy.
    The free trade debate: reports of the Twentieth Century Fund Task Force on the Future of American Trade Policy.
        p.   cm.
    "Background paper by Gary Clyde Hufbauer"
    Includes bibliographical references.
    1. United States—Commercial policy. 2. Uruguay Round (1987–   ) 3. Free trade—United States.
I. Hufbauer, Gary Clyde. II. Twentieth Century Fund. Task Force on the Future of American Trade Policy.
HF1455.F743   1989   382'.71'0973   89-70019
ISBN 0-87078-308-4   CIP
ISBN 0-87078-309-2 (pbk.)

Foreword

The economics and politics of trade policy have become a hotly debated issue in the United States. One need only look at the persistent, immense trade deficit of this country to understand the intensity of the argument. American jobs, financial stability, and prestige are at stake. Most political figures have had to make some adjustments to these facts of life.

The Twentieth Century Fund decided to establish an independent Task Force to examine issues related to American trade policy and to make recommendations for the future. Gary Clyde Hufbauer, Wallenberg Professor of International Financial Diplomacy at Georgetown University, was selected to write the background paper. Mr. Hufbauer is to be commended for his work in an area of great complexity and political sensitivity.

The Fund seeks, in general, to achieve a consensus in the Task Force process. We bring together people with diverse views in the hope of finding common ground for policy recommendations. In this case, however, the Task Force members elected to present two signed reports, one generally supporting free trade, the other suggesting other approaches to trade policy. The result mirrors the divisions among even the most knowledgeable on these difficult issues.

The Fund, of course, understands the members' adherence to their strong beliefs and thanks them for their efforts to sort through and debate these difficult issues.

Richard C. Leone, DIRECTOR
The Twentieth Century Fund
November 1989

Contents

Members of the Task Force

Anne Krueger, *chair*
Professor of Economics, Duke University
Consultant, World Bank

Lawrence J. Brainard
Senior Vice President, Bankers Trust Company

Patrick D. Choate
Vice President for Policy Analysis, TRW Inc.

Harry L. Freeman
Executive Vice President, Corporate Affairs and
   Communications, American Express Company

Paul Krugman
Professor of Economics, Massachusetts Institute of Technology

Robert Kuttner
Economics Editor, *The New Republic*

Robert Z. Lawrence
Senior Fellow, The Brookings Institution

Clyde V. Prestowitz
Senior Associate, The Carnegie Endowment

Howard D. Samuel
President, Industrial Union Department, AFL-CIO

Herbert Stein
Senior Fellow, The American Enterprise Institute

Alan Wm. Wolff, Esq.
Attorney, Dewey, Ballantine, Bushby, Palmer and Wood

Gary Clyde Hufbauer, *rapporteur*
Professor, School of Foreign Service, Georgetown University

REPORTS OF THE
TASK FORCE

The Case for Free Trade*

By the end of World War II, the international economic system had virtually disintegrated. Trade barriers were sky-high, it was practically impossible to move capital between countries, and links between multinational firms were severed. But the disastrous economic failures of the 1930s, followed by the cataclysmic trauma of the war, cleared the stage for radical reform.

The United States and the United Kingdom sponsored new institutions that led to the renewal of economic integration on every front. The International Monetary Fund and the Organisation for European Economic Cooperation (later the Organization for Economic Cooperation and Development, [OECD]) worked to dismantle exchange controls and capital barriers; the United States, operating through the Marshall Plan, bilateral aid, and the International Bank for Reconstruction and Development (later the World Bank), extended huge loans to Europe and Japan and then to Third World countries; multinational firms spread Western business methods across the globe; and, with the 1957 Treaty of Rome, Europe began to forge a continental economy.

Meanwhile, under auspices of the General Agreement on Tariffs and Trade (GATT), tariff barriers were slashed,

---

*The signatories to this Report, which was written by Gary Clyde Hufbauer, are Ms. Krueger and Messrs. Brainard, Freeman, Krugman, Lawrence, and Stein.

quantitative restrictions were eased, and trade expansion served as a great engine of postwar world growth. In addition, trade expansion was boosted by rapidly falling costs of communication and transportation. Between 1950 and 1980, the ratio of exports to Gross National Product (GNP) for the industrial countries rose from 7.4 percent to 16.7 percent, and per capita income nearly tripled. Many newly industrial countries—such as Singapore, South Korea, and Hong Kong—also produced and exported their way to far higher standards of living.

Thus, with enthusiastic American support, a golden age of trade, investment, and growth began. The trade agenda was erected on the economic precepts articulated by Adam Smith and David Ricardo: Free trade enables each country to specialize in those goods and services it produces best; it breaks down local monopolies, ensuring lower prices for consumers; and by promoting international competition, it spurs firms to innovate.

The classical Ricardian case for free trade does not depend on the policies of other countries. If a country's trading partners embrace free trade, so much the better, but unilateral free trade serves each country's own self-interest even if its trading partners choose to protect their own markets. This proposition is particularly evident in the case of raw materials. For example, it makes no sense for the United States to restrict imports of coffee, even if Brazil forbids imports of automobiles. As a corollary to this argument, the Ricardian model holds that a country should not be concerned with the composition of national output. If Japan closes its markets to cut lumber, thereby foreclosing exports by U.S. sawmills, the United States should not compound the ensuing inefficiency by prohibiting the export of logs—except as a tactical measure to prompt a rethinking of policy in Japan.

This tactical caveat explains why unilateral trade liberalization was not the formula devised for GATT negotiations in the postwar era. Instead, for reasons of domestic and international political arithmetic, concessions were given for concessions received. The formula of reciprocal concessions enlisted widespread business support for the GATT process. The reciprocal strategy enabled greater world economic efficiency than might have been possible with unilateral liberalization, but it was not strictly followed. The United States took the lead. Motivated by large trade surpluses as well as by classical teachings, the United States liberalized its market somewhat ahead of Europe, well ahead of Japan, and to a far greater extent than most developing countries.

THE CURRENT ENVIRONMENT
FOR TRADE POLICY

The world economic landscape of 1990 differs dramatically from the landscape of 1950. One consequence is that—despite the overwhelming success of the postwar agenda for the international economy and despite the intellectual underpinnings of the case for free trade—the American people are no longer confident that past policy themes will best serve American interests in the 1990s. Why the doubt? Several reasons can be listed:*

- In 1950, Japan was less than one-twentieth the economic size of the United States, and the twelve countries now in the European Community combined had an economy only half the size of that of the United States. Now Japan is half the size of the United States in economic terms, while the European Community and the United States are about equal. Meanwhile, the share

---

*In our view, many of these reasons wither under scrutiny, but they are often cited in the press and in the Congress as justification for a new approach to trade policy.

of U.S. GNP accounted for by exports of goods and services has grown from 5.0 percent to 9.5 percent. Because Europe and Japan are so much larger than before in relative terms, and because U.S. prosperity depends to a greater extent on the world economy, the United States now finds it burdensome to act as an economic buffer for the world trading system.

• Japan and Europe have also caught up with the United States in terms of living standards, and many Japanese and European firms are larger, better financed, and equally as innovative as their U.S. counterparts. The United States accordingly needs to pay more attention to trade concessions that might enable Japan and Europe to pull ahead of the United States in an absolute sense.

• High-technology products, such as the next generation of civilian aircraft and the 16-megabit semiconductor chip, require huge research and development (R&D) outlays. A firm can risk these outlays only if it can anticipate a very large market. The firm with a big, protected home market thus enjoys a tremendous advantage in developing new products.

• When an industry such as steel or apparel goes into decline, severe economic pain is often visited on displaced workers and depressed communities. Since federal programs for addressing economic dislocation are poorly funded and badly administered, restrictive trade measures may seem like a reasonable second-best policy.

• Many countries practice a greater degree of industrial intervention than the United States. On the one hand, intervention may give their high-tech firms a leg up (NTT in Japan and Airbus in Europe are often cited); on the other hand, intervention might shift adjustment burdens in declining industries to the United States (textiles and steel are illustrative).

Faced with the apparent competitive realities of the 1980s, which mark a decisive break from the golden age of the 1950s through the 1970s, U.S. trade policy has now reached a crossroads. Broadly speaking, five schools of thought can be distinguished in the public debate:

1. With limited exceptions, trade liberalization by the United States is good policy, even if not reciprocated by foreign countries.[1]

2. Trade liberalization by the United States is good policy, but only if reciprocated by foreign countries.[2]

3. Threats of new U.S. restrictions are sometimes desirable to achieve a more level playing field, even if, from time to time, the net result is higher barriers all around.

4. Because some important trading nations choose to manage important sectors of their economies, the United States has no choice but to accommodate this policy style and manage the same sectors in the U.S. economy.

5. Whatever other countries may do, a more restrictive stance by the United States would be desirable in some sectors.

The Task Force members who have signed this report advocate one or another of the first three propositions—unilateral liberalization with limited exceptions, reciprocal concessions, and the threat of restrictions. The members reject the last two propositions—accommodation to foreign styles of industrial policy and selective unilateral restrictions.

We contend that, on the whole, established approaches to trade policy have worked well, that the United States should concentrate on domestic measures to improve economic performance, and that continued rapid liberalization on a reciprocal basis represents the best trade policy consistent with U.S.-self-interest.

To be sure, we are concerned about the dynamics of international liberalization. What should determine the pace and scale of U.S. concessions in response to concessions received? Will U.S. threats lead to trade wars or general economic disarmament? Will industrial policy abroad provide our trading partners with an irrevocable lead in "strategic" industries? We are confident that, with proper domestic policies, U.S. firms can hold their own in strategic industries. We also believe that the United States has many valuable bargaining chips of great interest to Europe and Japan, such as improved access to the U.S. financial services markets, airline landing rights, and high-tech government procurement.

Putting aside the tactics of liberalization, *the Task Force believes that relatively free trade within a world system of common rules should continue to serve as the guiding star of U.S. policy.* This goal is not only right for the United States; it is also right for the world economy. The reality is that it is still up to the United States not only to look after its own interests but also to provide leadership for improving the world trading system. U.S. concerns about trade barriers, therefore, should extend to Japanese restrictions against agricultural imports from Australia and Thailand and industrial imports from most developing nations; to European restrictions against a range of imports both from Japan and the developing nations; and even to Indian restrictions on imports from Hong Kong. At the same time, the United States should discourage "export targeting" throughout the world trading system—that is, the practice of subsidizing favored industries by some countries to capture an abnormal share of the open world market.

All nations will benefit from multilateral liberalization as well as from trading patterns consistent with the laws of comparative advantage. The question is how to get there from here. Which approaches will enlist the support of the U.S. Congress, which will prompt other countries to liberalize their own markets on a multilateral basis, which will meet the challenge of export targeting?

President Bush is faced with a series of decisions on a variety of trade conflicts, which, once made, will add up to a trade strategy. Over the next two years, the Bush administration must decide the balance between results-oriented arrangements and free market approaches in such key sectors as semiconductors, steel, and telecommunications. The administration must combine the new emphasis on unilateral "crowbars" to secure trade concessions from foreign countries—exemplified by the telecommunications provisions and "Super 301" in the 1988 Trade Act—with a more traditional emphasis on opening the U.S. market as an incentive for foreign nations to open theirs. The administration must decide how much support to accord U.S. export promotion programs such as the Export-Import Bank, the Foreign Sales Corporation tax incentives, and Sematech and other research consortia. And the administration must balance the diplomatic effort it dedicates to the Uruguay Round of multilateral GATT negotiations against narrower dealings with the European Community and Japan.

The Trade Deficit

An important constraint on President Bush's freedom to shape policy is the U.S. trade deficit.[3] Most of the members who have signed this report see the deficit as a cause for concern on both economic and political grounds.*

---

*Some of us believe that the trade deficit is, at most, an economic and political distraction. In this view, nothing is lost if the United States imports more than it exports, nor if foreigners correspondingly choose to invest in U.S. securities and factories. The trade deficit may reflect inadequate U.S. savings, but that problem—if it is a problem—should be addressed through smaller federal budget deficits and larger private savings, not by handwringing over the trade deficit.

In the long run, the continuing trade deficit facilitates the accumulation by foreigners of U.S. assets on a large scale. Apart from political questions of "who owns America," large foreign holdings will result in significant future payments of investment income to foreigners, in amounts that may ultimately impair the U.S. standard of living. Further, the trade deficit creates U.S. dependence on foreign central banks and private investors to finance the United States, with the attendant risk that, if these financiers suddenly changed their minds, the outrush of capital could destabilize the world economy. Most importantly, we fear that a continuing large trade deficit will serve both to legitimize calls for restricting U.S. imports of manufactured goods and to reinforce the emphasis on unilateral retaliation and managed trade.

We believe that the major causes of the U.S. trade deficit have a macroeconomic character: namely, savings and investment imbalances in the United States and abroad, particularly in Europe and Japan. These imbalances reflect the varying fiscal deficits and surpluses, and different private savings and investment levels, both within and between the major trading countries. If the public and private imbalances are corrected, and if exchange rates move appropriately to redirect demand between the traded and nontraded sectors in each country, then disproportionately large trade deficits and surpluses can be reduced. Ideally, this means that the United States should save more (both publicly and privately) while Europe and Japan should invest more; and, at the same time, the dollar should fall relative to the mark and the yen.*

---

*Some of us contend that the broad macroeconomic developments of the 1980s do not entirely explain the roller-coaster ride of the dollar—first an appreciation of over 40 percent between 1980 and 1985, then an extended decline. Even though the dollar has practically come back to its 1980 starting

(continued on next page)

Trade policy on its own can make little if any dent in the trade deficit. This is not to say that foreign barriers are unimportant, but they are normally too limited in their sweep to affect the broad national balance of savings and investment. For example, if Japan suddenly opened its supercomputer, rice, lumber, mobile telephone, and other closed markets, what would happen to the U.S trade deficit? In the first instance, U.S. exports to Japan might shoot up, say by $5 billion annually. But unless the expansion of U.S. imports were accompanied by an equivalent $5 billion fall in the Japanese savings/investment balance, and a corresponding $5 billion rise in the U.S. savings/investment balance, the exchange markets would soon counteract the initial $5 billion boost in U.S. exports. Specifically, the yen would depreciate and the dollar would appreciate just enough to restore the old trade balance. The U.S. terms of trade would improve—an important gain for the United States. The composition of U.S. output would change: more supercomputers, rice, lumber, and mobile telephones produced and exported, accompanied by less production and exportation of a great many other goods and services. But the U.S. trade balance would remain much as before.

THE GOALS OF THE U.S. TRADE POLICY

Leaving aside the trade deficit, the real and important purposes of trade policy are fourfold:

---

point, and even though the U.S. economy is near the same level of capacity utilization, the U.S. trade deficit remains above $100 billion. By comparison, in 1980 the trade deficit was approximately $25 billion. What happened in the meantime? Why does the same exchange rate coupled with the same level of aggregate demand not produce approximately the same trade balance? One answer is that U.S. product quality and process technology have slipped relative to the United States' industrial competitors.

1. Trade policy can raise national efficiency by reallocating resources to more productive activities and by broadening consumer choice.

2. Trade policy can open foreign markets to U.S. goods and services, thereby improving the terms of trade (the price of exports relative to the price of imports). This is important: If, by opening foreign markets, trade policy could avert a 5 percent depreciation of the dollar, the income gains to the United States would be $15 to $20 billion annually (about 0.4 percent of GNP).

3. Trade policy can ensure that U.S. firms enjoy equal competitive opportunities on world markets so that they can spread their overhead and R&D costs over a larger production base. The alternative is that U.S. firms may not be able to pursue new technologies that may cost $100 million, $500 million, or more to develop.

4. The United States has a decisive leadership role to play in the evolution of the world trading system. Even though the European Community equals the United States in terms of economic size, the European Community is too preoccupied with internal questions to lead the world trading system; and Japan is not only smaller, it also shows little disposition to step into a leadership role. For better or worse, the approaches propounded by the United States stand the best chance of adoption by the world trading system.

THREE CRITICAL ISSUES

National Differences in the Organization of Trade Policy

Realization of the goals of trade policy sometimes conflicts with systemic national differences in the organization of trade policy. National differences make it difficult for the big economic powers to find common ground, even with vigorous U.S. leadership.

The United States advocates clear trade policies formulated according to well-defined rules. This approach has not made the United States a free trading nation, but its trade laws, including the Trade Act of 1988, have created an accountable and open system. When the United States does restrict imports, it sets explicit quantitative limits or tariffs that are visible for all to see. Barriers are created or changed only after public proceedings. Finally, most U.S. trade restraints take the form of limitations "voluntarily" imposed by foreign suppliers on their own exports. This style enables foreign producers to capture the "quota rents" that are created by artificial scarcity in the U.S. market.[4]

As one consequence of a transparent and open system, the United States buys an exceptional share of developing-country manufactured exports to developed nations—in 1987, some 57 percent of the total. In 1988, the United States imported over 300,000 Hyundai autos from South Korea; the European Community imported 21,000 and Japan only 150. Even in the steel sector, where the United States does maintain import restrictions, the U.S. level of import penetration is 20 percent, compared with 10 percent for the European Community and 7 percent for Japan.*

Other industrial countries do not rely to the same extent as the United States on detailed legal mechanisms; instead, they formulate trade policy with large helpings of ministerial discretion. The result is often a web of invisible barriers. In this connection, Japan presents special problems. Japan has established a brilliant postwar record

---

*Some of us question whether such examples demonstrate that the U.S. market is more open than the European or Japanese markets. In each case, other factors may explain the discrepancy, and, in unnamed instances, the United States may be more restrictive.

of economic growth, accompanied by a pervasive system of managed trade. Yet Japan still regards itself as a developing state, where trade policy is part of a broad public/private strategy for industrial advance. Some of the Japanese practices that rankle U.S. and European firms today (for example, in the area of supercomputers and satellites) stem from continuing restrictive government policies, but most of the objectionable practices are credited to an economic system that stresses durable relations between purchasers and supplier firms and tolerates cartel behavior among competing firms.

Meanwhile, the contributions of the Japanese government to the world trading system are not always commensurate with its global economic power. Unlike the United States in the 1950s and 1960s, Japan does not gladly give more trade concessions than it receives in multilateral negotiations. In fact, Japan has reduced its trade barriers only when faced with extreme pressure from foreign powers, notably the United States and more recently the European Community.

The U.S. and Japanese approaches to trade policy have far less in common than the European and U.S. approaches, but the European Community and the United States still differ on industrial policy. We fear that Europe 1992 may contain important elements of managed trade, not only in high-tech products (semiconductors, telecommunications, satellites, and civilian aircraft) where government procurement and research consortia play a major role, but also in more mundane but politically sensitive industries (agriculture and steel).

Considering these important national differences, the members of the Task Force who have signed this report have reached several conclusions. As a starting point, *a world system of consistently applied rules and approaches would help maintain civilized relationships among trading nations and set the stage for the gradual removal of bar-*

riers and distortions, for the creation of level playing fields,
and for the establishment of a more open world economy.

Sector Arrangements

Two reports have been issued by the members of this
Task Force because the members found themselves in
disagreement over the merits of rules-oriented and results-
oriented approaches, particularly on a sector-by-sector
basis.[5] Some Task Force members emphasized that no
elaboration of rules would dissuade Belgium from subsidizing Sabena and otherwise ensuring the continued existence of its national airline. Nor would major European
nations be dissuaded from supporting Airbus to whatever
extent is necessary to compete with Boeing (possibly, in
the process, pushing McDonnell Douglas out of the civilian
aircraft market). Nor would Japan be deterred from pursuing the supercomputer and military aircraft industries,
even though U.S. products are available to Japan at much
lower cost.

In the view of those Task Force members, energetic U.S.
efforts to change dedicated industrial strategies abroad
will simply engender rancor and resentment and harm the
United States' overall relationships with important
economic and political allies. In their view, results-oriented
managed trade must form an important part of the U.S.
response. Well-designed sector agreements can partly insulate the U.S. economy from aggressive Japanese and
European export practices—industrial targeting, subsidiza-
tion, and dumping—and, when political circumstances are
right, such arrangements can pry open foreign markets
to U.S. exports.

Those of us who have signed "The Case for Free Trade"
disagree with this line of analysis. In fact, *we see great*
danger in a results-oriented approach applied to specific sec-
tors. In our view, sectoral groups are too often captured
by producers; a sectoral approach in steel can easily spread

to machine tools or other areas of production; and even implicit understandings on acceptable import levels will serve to diminish competitive forces, to the immediate disadvantage of U.S. consumers and to the long-term detriment of U.S. producers. One of the worst examples of sectoral protection is the sugar industry. U.S. sugar policy costs all U.S. consumers more than $1 billion annually through high sugar prices, while it generates profits for a few thousand U.S. producers. Meanwhile, it has devastated the economies of many countries, notably in the Caribbean, leaving them even more prone to drug traffickers and less able to deal with their external debt. And, ironically, it has encouraged corn sweetener producers to take over the domestic U.S. sugar market from sugarcane and beet growers. The best news on the sugar front, in our view, is that a recent GATT panel found U.S. practices inconsistent with U.S. obligations to the GATT, a finding that could pave the way for reform.

The case of sugar is bad but not unique. Sectorally managed trade often backfires; many "voluntary" restraint agreements (VRAs) have weakened the protected U.S. industries by adding profits to the ledger sheets of their foreign and domestic competitors. Steel restraints enlarged the profits of integrated steel producers in South Korea and Canada, as well as minimills in the United States. Automobile restraints paved the way for Toyota and Nissan to become major producers in the U.S. market.

We believe that the right approach is to stress and formulate rules of the playing field, and to stay away from indicative market shares and other results-oriented frameworks except as a last resort. Rules may be difficult and frustrating to negotiate, but often yield better results. For example, between 1985 and 1987, U.S. exports to Japan in four sectors that were the subject of intense negotiations—pharmaceuticals and medical equipment, electronics, forest products, and telecommunications—rose by 47 percent, twice the growth rate of total U.S. exports to Japan.

The basic disagreement between the signatories to this Report and those who have signed the other when it comes to the role of sector policy can be summarized as follows: We do not accept the premise that sectoral strategies will continue abroad for a very long time, notably in Japan and in high-technology industries. Nor do we believe that such policies, if not matched, will capture "strategic" industries and relegate the United States to second-class industrial status. Instead, we are convinced that foreign countries, including Japan, will abide by general rules sooner rather than later, particularly if the United States provides leadership in articulating these rules. *We believe that the United States will only damage its own economic strength by emulating the industrial management policies that are pursued in Japan and elsewhere.* We question the ability of any government to choose "strategic" industries wisely.

Aggressive Reciprocity

The unilateral approach to trade policy was highlighted in May 1989 by the designation of unfair trading partners (notably Japan, Brazil, and India) under Super 301 of the 1988 Trade Act. Some members of the Task Force see such measures, with the ultimate threat of retaliation, as an appropriate response to the "rocky coast" conditions of foreign countries. By forcefully responding to foreign barriers, the United States not only accelerates the opening of foreign markets but also curbs sentiment for closing domestic markets. According to this analysis, the use of tough tactics by a world leader can eventually lead to a more open global trading system than a conciliatory strategy.

Decades of GATT negotiations have conditioned nations to think that exports are good and imports are bad, but that the benefit flowing from exports outweighs the harm resulting from imports. In seven rounds of multilateral trade negotiations, this mode of "GATT think" was implemented by reciprocal concessions, to the mutual advantage of all countries, importers as well as exporters. Now, however, tough tactics may be needed to carry out the same task of reducing barriers. As support for this hypothesis, note that Japan recently opened its mobile telephone market under U.S. pressure and that Super 301 has prompted a flurry of liberalization in South Korea and Taiwan and much interest by many nations in the Uruguay Round of trade negotiations.[6]

The signatories to this report believe that the new emphasis on unilateral retaliation will ultimately erode political support for an open trading system. Powerful trading areas, notably the United States and the European Community, may come to see retaliation as an acceptable alternative to mutual reduction of barriers. Unilateral tools may come to be misused by interest groups seeking to insulate themselves from foreign competition. And the threat of retaliation could easily spark antagonism in target countries and harden resistance to trade liberalization. Based on this analysis, the United States should place far greater stress on reciprocal multilateral concessions than on unilateral retaliation.

One possible reconciliation between the advocates of liberalization and the skeptics could emerge from the Uruguay Round talks. The major trading nations could well agree to new rules covering a wider range of subjects—financial services, intellectual property, subsidy practices—coupled with more expeditious dispute settlement procedures. In return, the United States could channel its complaints through GATT panels in areas where agreed rules exist, and, when it took unilateral steps in other areas, the United States could abandon the practice of retaliatory measures that are found to violate GATT norms.

FREE TRADE AREAS AND COMMON MARKETS

We believe that free trade areas and common markets offer a promising approach for the development of agreed rules and the eventual removal of behind-the-border distortions.[7] One of the most constructive accomplishments of the Reagan administration was the negotiation of a landmark free trade arrangement with Canada. The dramatic results of the common market approach are particularly evident in the Europe 1992 process and the Australia-New Zealand Closer Economic Relations Agreement. Such groupings have proved robust largely because they are created on the basis of a high political comfort level among participating countries that enables each participant to surrender some degree of economic sovereignty and accept common regulation of behind-the-border practices.

The danger inherent in large free trade areas and common markets is that they may fragment the world trading system into regional blocs. For example, once the European Community completes the Europe 1992 process, it may focus its energies on absorbing certain members of the European Free Trade Association, notably Austria and Norway, and building commercial links with Eastern Europe. Meanwhile, the United States and Canada could concentrate on enlarging their free trade area to include Mexico. And Japan might strengthen its informal investment and trade ties with Thailand, Hong Kong, Taiwan, South Korea, and China. The net result of such efforts might be freer trade within the areas but also greater divisions between the blocs.

There is one clear way to reap the advantages of the common market approach, with its elimination of behind-the-border barriers, while avoiding the fragmentation of the world trading system. *We believe that after the Uruguay Round, an OECD-plus common market, encompassing present OECD members and new arrivals, should be the target for the year 2000.* This area would create a common institutional framework among the major powers that would gradually break down a wide variety of behind-the-border barriers—different safety, environmental, and technical standards; different antitrust policies; different tax systems; and restrictive national procurement practices.

At the same time, no member of the OECD-plus common market would raise its border barriers against nonmembers. Instead, all members would pledge to eventually reduce their border barriers to the lowest prevailing level. This principle alone would ensure that Japan and Europe ultimately open their markets to manufactured goods from the developing nations to the same extent that the United States already has.

On a practical note, we caution that it will prove far easier to work out common rules across the Atlantic with the European Community, and across the South Pacific with Australia and New Zealand, than across the North Pacific with Japan and South Korea.

Whatever approaches may prove appealing after 1991, at this juncture the most urgent matter is successful completion of the Uruguay Round. In earlier decades, propelled by energetic U.S. leadership, the GATT system chalked up many accomplishments: It helped facilitate an enormous expansion in trade, mainly by creating rules to promote freer trade while allowing countries to safeguard their vital industries; it provided external reference points to distinguish between impermissible unfair trade practices and permissible, even if different, fair trade practices; and its commitments served as a bulwark against domestic pressure groups. Notwithstanding this distinguished record, the GATT system is now held in low esteem by the U.S. Congress, business, and labor.

The diminished stature of the GATT and the slow pace of the Uruguay Round partly mirror the fact that the natural domain for GATT has been tariffs and other border barriers, rather than opaque, behind-the-border measures such as tied distribution systems and discriminatory technical standards. In fact, GATT negotiations often open markets only in legal terms, not in terms of practical access, because behind-the-border barriers continue to thwart foreign suppliers.

Nevertheless, *the members of the Task Force who have signed this report strongly urge the Bush administration to concentrate its immediate efforts on the Uruguay Round of GATT talks.* Even though the United States now accounts for a smaller share of world production and trade, U.S. leadership can still be decisive. The Uruguay Round offers the last, best chance to convert the GATT into an effective instrument for creating a global trade regime—agriculture, financial services, intellectual property, government procurement, and a whole range of other issues described in the background paper accompanying this Report. If the GATT system is now strengthened—for example, through a larger secretariat, an increased budget, and improved surveillance procedures—it can act as an objective watchdog over national trade practices.

But *we believe that in order for the GATT talks to achieve any degree of success, the United States must be prepared to make concessions to receive concessions.* For example, it should offer:

- More liberal trade in sugar, dairy, and meat products, and limitations on price-support programs and other agricultural subsidies;
- Phaseout of the restrictive VRAs on steel, in parallel with the abandonment of dumping and subsidy practices by other trading nations and the opening of European and Japanese markets to imports;
- Gradual liberalization of trade in textiles and apparel, again in a broad international context;
- More open access to government procurement, in-

cluding military procurement (from U.S. allies) and state
government procurement;
• A multilateral overview of the Section 301 process
and some limitations on the U.S. antidumping laws.

In return for such concessions, the United States can
expect:

• Far more open markets in agriculture and government procurement on a worldwide basis;
• An end to import licensing regimes, sky-high tariffs,
and other barriers by the newly industrial economies,
such as South Korea, Thailand, Malaysia, Argentina,
and Brazil;
• Genuinely improved access to numerous Japanese
markets, ranging from rice to lumber to semiconductors
to financial services;
• Much better protection for copyrights, patents, and
trademarks in a great many countries;
• A GATT regime of rules for trade in services built
on the cornerstone of equitable national treatment for
foreign firms and the right of establishment;
• Much stronger GATT machinery for surveillance of
trade policies and settlement of disputes.

This seems a worthwhile bargain. A major success in the
Uruguay Round will ensure the integrity of the global
trading system, improve U.S. efficiency, and stimulate
world growth.

Whatever the outcome of the Uruguay Round, the Bush
administration should begin thinking about the post-1991
agenda. Left to its own momentum, in the 1990s the world
trading system is likely to fragment into three major
blocs—one led by the United States, one led by Japan, and
one led by the European Community. To avert this outcome, and to preserve the benefits of an integrated world

trading system, *the Task Force strongly recommends that concrete plans be prepared for OECD-wide talks on a far-reaching and open-ended common market.*

NOTES

1. The exceptions include industries that must be preserved at home for national security reasons and instances where it is clear that reciprocal concessions can soon be attained by temporarily maintaining U.S. trade barriers.

2. Concessions by other countries need not affect the same sector as concessions by the United States. For example, if the United States liberalized sugar imports, Brazil might liberalize computer imports, and Australia might liberalize automobiles.

3. The term "trade deficit" is used here as a shorthand expression for the current account deficit. The current account deficit reflects not only the balance of merchandise trade but also the balance of business services (such as transportation and tourism) and the balance of investment income (such as interest, dividends, and royalties).

4. For example, in June 1989 the price of sugar in the protected U.S. market was $0.23 per pound, while the price in the open world market was $0.10 per pound. Foreign suppliers who held quota privileges to sell sugar in the U.S. market thereby earned $0.13 per pound "quota rent" over the world price.

5. The terms "rules-oriented" and "results-oriented" are shorthand. Those who advocate a rules-oriented approach maintain that concrete results will flow—namely, more multilateral trade governed by the laws of comparative advantage. Those who advocate a results-oriented approach are not unmindful of the need for sensible rules, but they want the results to be specified in harmony with the laws of comparative advantage.

6. In the Tokyo Round of multilateral trade negotiations (1973-79), the U.S. countervailing duty laws provided a major impetus for talks on subsidies and other issues. In the Uruguay Round (1986-91?), Super 301 of the 1988 Trade Act could play the same role. The "rogue elephant" aspect of U.S. trade behavior might prove decisive in prodding the Uruguay Round

to reach a successful conclusion on services, intellectual property, and other new areas.

7. Technically speaking, in a free trade area, the participants eliminate tariffs and other border barriers between themselves, but each participant maintains its own barriers against the rest of the world. In a common market, the participants not only eliminate barriers between themselves but also devise common tariffs and other barriers against the rest of the world. As a dramatic further step, the nations in a common market may harmonize their internal economic regulations and thereby eliminate behind-the-border barriers. This is the process that the twelve nations of the European Community have embarked upon, known as Europe 1992.

A Fresh Look at Trade Policy*

At first glance, it appears that there is little reason for the United States to significantly change its trade and economic policies. At home, the economy is enjoying its longest period of expansion since World War II, unemployment is hovering around 5 percent, and inflation has not become a serious problem. Abroad, the output of industrial countries grew by 4.1 percent in 1988, while the volume of world trade expanded by 9.3 percent. This seemingly rosy picture helps explain the current administration's quiescence on trade and international economic issues, and the short shrift given to trade matters at the July 1989 summit of the seven major industrialized countries.

The members of the Task Force who have signed this Report believe that the "if it ain't broke, don't fix it" mentality is mistaken. Chronic trade imbalances threaten the stability of the world economy, the United States faces serious challenges to its economic leadership, and the multilateral trading system is clearly in need of modernization. *We believe that, although trade policy cannot eliminate the global economic imbalances or restore our international competitiveness, it can make a contribution toward these goals.*

---

*The signatories to this Report are Messrs. Choate, Kuttner, Prestowitz, Samuel, and Wolff.

WHY A TRADE POLICY?

Trade Imbalances

The United States has had unprecedented current account deficits of over $100 billion for the past five years (the 1988 deficit was $136.4 billion). By contrast, as recently as 1981 the United States had a current account surplus of $6.8 billion. William Cline of the Institute for International Economics has predicted that the current account deficit could rise to roughly $200 billion by 1992. Mirroring the U.S. deficits are the surpluses of Japan, West Germany, and the East Asian newly industrializing countries. (In 1988, these surpluses were $79.5 billion, $48.3 billion, and $31.6 billion, respectively.)

These imbalances are troublesome for several reasons. First, the U.S. trade deficit has led to job loss in export- and import-competing industries, sectors that tend to pay higher wages. Second, the deficit has transformed the United States from the world's largest creditor (+$141.1 billion in 1981) to the world's largest debtor (–$532.5 billion in 1988). Although foreign borrowing is not intrinsically harmful, the debt has not been used to finance additional productive investment. As a result, the standard of living of future generations of Americans will suffer as a growing percentage of our GNP is diverted to meet the interest payments on our foreign debt.

Finally, these imbalances threaten the stability of the world economy. If foreign investors stopped financing the U.S. current account deficit, the dollar could fall precipitously and sharply higher interest rates could exacerbate the Third World debt crisis and push the world economy into a recession. This "hard landing" scenario may not come to pass: The U.S. trade deficit absorbs an increasingly smaller portion of world savings, and the central banks have stepped up their purchase of dollar-denominated assets when foreign private investors were unwilling to buy them. Given the high stakes involved, however, the United States should not continue to depend on the kindness of strangers.

Although some dollar devaluation may be necessary to reduce the U.S. current account deficit, devaluation imposes substantial costs on the U.S. standard of living. The United States should focus on measures (such as increased U.S. productivity, increased domestic demand in the surplus countries, and greater access to foreign markets) that will reduce global trade imbalances without driving wages down.

U.S. Industrial and Technological Leadership

The U.S. position in basic and leading-edge industries continues to erode. The U.S. trade balance in manufactured goods slipped from a surplus of $15.5 billion in 1981 to a deficit of $119.1 billion in 1988. The U.S. surplus in high-technology goods fell from $31 billion to $6 billion over the same period. From 1970 to 1987, U.S. companies' share of the domestic market declined from 90 percent to 10 percent for color televisions, 90 percent to 1 percent for phonographs, and 100 percent to 35 percent for machining centers. Videocassette recorders, facsimile machines, liquid crystal displays, and compact disc players are no longer produced by U.S. firms. Japanese firms now control nearly 90 percent of the market for advanced memory devices. The U.S. supercomputer industry has recently been rocked by the exit of Control Data and the split-up of Cray Research into two separate companies. The United States also continues to fall behind in critical technologies and products of the future: X-ray lithography, superconductivity, biotechnology, manufacturing automation, and high-definition television.

Many of the reasons for the erosion of U.S. competitiveness in manufacturing and high-technology industries can be found right here at home: inadequate investment in plant and equipment and civilian research and development, the high cost of capital, and an unhealthy emphasis on financial engineering and short-term profits—to name only a few.

Even if these problems were corrected, the United States would still have to face the fact that capitalism comes in a wide variety of national flavors. Some of our trading partners adopt conscious polices to promote strategic industries. In other high-technology sectors, our entrepreneurial start-ups do not seem to have the staying power of their large, vertically integrated competitors. Rather than sweeping these problems under the rug, the United States must develop a trade policy that recognizes the differences in the industrial systems and policies of our competitors.

A Rickety Multilateral Trading System

As a result of seven rounds of multilateral trade negotiations under the General Agreement on Tariffs and Trade (GATT), average tariffs in industrial countries on industrial products fell from over 40 percent in 1947 to roughly 5 percent today, while the volume of world trade in manufactured goods expanded twentyfold.

Recently, it has become fashionable to say that the GATT is in danger of being swept into the dustbin of history. Some analysts believe that blocs (the European Community, North America, and the Pacific Rim) will become increasingly important to the management of international trade. Others point to the rise in "gray-area" export restraint agreements, which increased from 135 in September 1987 to 261 in May 1988. Still others decry the GATT's weak dispute settlement mechanism and the wide range of economic activity that is not covered (effectively or at all) by GATT, including agriculture, services, intellectual property, and investment measures.

THE STATE OF THE DEBATE

After World War II, the United States constructed the GATT as a world trade and payments system based on multilateralism, nondiscrimination, and the progressive reduction of barriers to the flow of goods and capital.[1] This system contributed to the rapid increase in world trade and the fourfold increase in world real income between 1950 and 1985.

In the past, the United States was willing to make asymmetric trade concessions; during the first twenty years of the GATT, the United States gave roughly two scheduled concessions for every one that it received. At the time, the United States placed much more emphasis on the political-military objective of rebuilding the economies of its allies than on its own commercial and economic interests. The United States could afford to be generous, since the most sophisticated products were invented and produced in the United States.

Over the years, the basic commitment of the United States to trade liberalization has not changed. "Free trade" is thought to increase economic efficiency by (a) allowing nations to exploit increasing returns to scale in a larger market, (b) permitting specialization in accordance with comparative advantage, and (c) encouraging innovation as a result of stiffer competition. U.S. industries are occasionally protected, but generally only as a response to foreign unfair trade practices and/or politics.

The center of gravity has changed with respect to "reciprocity." As a result of the huge U.S. trade deficits and declining U.S. competitiveness, Congress has pressured recent administrations to combat more aggressively those foreign barriers that reduce exports of U.S. goods and services. This change in circumstances is responsible for some of the major provisions of the Omnibus Trade and Competitiveness Act of 1988. In addition to "Super

301," which requires the president to initiate negotiations on the "priority" unfair trade practices of "priority" countries, the bill contains reciprocity provisions for telecommunications, intellectual property protection, and government procurement.

Debate continues to take place on three fundamental questions: whether the United States must adopt different trade policies for trading partners with different industrial systems; how the United States should respond to foreign export targeting; and whether the United States should concentrate its energies on multilateral, plurilateral, bilateral, or unilateral trade policy approaches.

Tailored Trade Policies?

One important trade policy debate is whether the economies of our trading partners are so different as to necessitate different trade strategies. Japan is the country most often mentioned as being "unique." *Analysis of the U.S.-Japan Trade Problem,* the report of the Advisory Council on Trade Policy and Negotiations (ACTPN), touched off a heated debate when it advocated (after first citing the U.S. budget deficit as a pre-condition for any new policy) a "results-oriented trade strategy" to cope with Japan's invisible trade barriers such as the buying practices of its industrial groups. The report urged U.S. negotiators to "insist on appropriate sectoral import levels that properly reflect the international competitiveness of U.S. suppliers." The ACTPN panel felt this approach was necessary because Japan was an underimporter, and because many of the barriers (*keiretsu,* administrative guidance, the distribution system, anticompetitive practices) would be difficult to eliminate by Japanese commitments to improving procedures under the GATT or agreeing to new rules of behavior.

This "results-oriented" approach was criticized for several reasons:

- Sectoral, rules-based negotiations that deal with the multidimensional nature of Japanese protection have been successful. (For example, after the Japanese agreed to privatize the Japan Tobacco and Salt Corporation, eliminate high tariffs, and open distribution channels, U.S. exports of cigarettes increased from $76.2 million in 1985 to $606.3 million in 1988.)
- Trade agreements such as the automotive voluntary export restraints that focus on outcomes may be "captured" by narrow domestic interests at the expense of consumers, and may even redound to the advantage of the Japanese.
- Establishing import targets would increase government control over the Japanese economy—which is precisely what the United States wants to avoid. MITI would presumably organize import cartels to enforce the agreements.

The fact remains that, in some sectors, the "rules-based" approach has been tried and found wanting. The United States has tried to open up the Japanese semiconductor market for eighteen years, but as a result of restricted buying practices, U.S. producers have never been able to obtain more than a residual share of the Japanese market. Setting market-share objectives may be necessary on a transitional basis to push the market to operate more freely.

Industrial Strategies and International Trade

Much of the trade policy debate is really an argument over how to respond to foreign industrial policy. Traditionally, the United States has taken the view that government should have little or nothing to do with the sectoral composition of the economy (outside of defense, housing, agriculture, and space-related activities), since the market will allocate labor and capital to their most productive use.

Most of our competitors, however, have considered it a self-evident proposition that there is a national economic interest in developing certain industries. The debate over how to react to foreign industrial policy has become more heated in recent years because comparative advantage in some industries seems to have been "created" by the visible hand of the state rather than "revealed" by the invisible hand of the marketplace; the United States finds itself behind its competitors in industries judged by many to be important.

There is no consensus in trade policy circles as to the direction the U.S. response to foreign industrial targeting should take. A neoclassical economist would conclude that, if foreigners are foolish enough to export subsidized goods, we should take advantage of their generosity. Others believe that the United States should use its trade laws to try to get other nations to stop subsidizing or protecting their strategic industries; they would advocate sectoral agreements as a stopgap measure until a more liberal trading regime could be achieved.

Still another school of thought, prevalent in certain European countries, is that "free trade" in some sectors is neither realistic nor necessarily desirable, and that pragmatic alternatives must be devised. If all states feel the need to maintain a certain amount of self-sufficiency in a certain product, even though they may not be the low-cost producer, one alternative is to allow every country to reserve a certain share of its market for domestic producers and allow foreign producers to compete for the rest. This would recognize that states are likely to regard some market outcomes (the loss of a "critical" industry) as unacceptable, while trying to preserve some of the advantages of competitive markets.

Trade Policy Approaches:
Multi-, Pluri-, Bi-, or Uni-lateral?

Multi-, pluri-, bi-, and uni-lateral approaches to negotiating all have advocates and critics. The real question is which of these approaches is most ideally suited for which problems.

The GATT is regarded by some as a slow and ponderous process that will generate a "least common denominator" outcome. On the other hand, many of the world's trade problems are multilateral in nature and can only be solved in multilateral forums. It would also be much easier, and arguably more effective, to negotiate one universal agreement on trade-related intellectual property, for example, as opposed to myriad bilateral treaties.

Plurilateralism is useful if a group of like-minded nations is ready for rules, disciplines, and a level of economic integration for which not all ninety-two members of the GATT are prepared. This is the notion behind the Tokyo Round codes of the GATT, the European single market of 1992, and an "OECD-plus common market," which would eventually extend harmonization from trade and monetary affairs to tax and competition policies.

Some analysts find the U.S.-Canada Free Trade Area model appealing and have proposed extending it to Japan, ASEAN, Taiwan, South Korea, and Mexico. Free trade areas are probably only useful in a limited number of circumstances (geographically contiguous countries with roughly the same level of economic development and barriers to trade caused mainly by border measures).

The United States has been frequently berated for being "unilateralist," especially in connection with its enforcement of the 1988 Trade Act. The United States stands accused of being "judge and jury," retaliating without dispensation from a GATT panel, and of stretching the boundaries of what is "unfair" beyond present limits.

Judicious use of unilateralist tactics, however, can open markets where no clear multilateral remedies exist, and can serve as an incentive for other countries to join multilateral trade agreements. Because the United States is the largest open economy in the world, continued access to its market is one of the few areas of leverage it has left.

POLICY RECOMMENDATIONS

The members of the Task Force who have signed this report believe that the United States should adopt the goal of attaining a trade surplus by 1993. The United States should set as a national goal the elimination of its current account deficit—preferably within the next four to five years. Achieving this will require changes in macroeconomic, structural, and trade policies here and abroad. *To achieve this goal, the United States must boost private savings and reduce the federal budget deficit, and in all likelihood, further depreciate the dollar against some currencies.* At the same time, the surplus countries must open their markets and rely on domestic-oriented growth.

The Bush administration's Structural Impediments Initiative could be a useful vehicle for addressing many of the factors that are contributing to Japan's chronic trade surpluses: tolerance of anticompetitive practices and housing and land-use policies that stifle consumption.

We also recommend that the United States respond effectively to foreign export targeting. Comparative advantage is no longer determined solely by the availability of land, labor, capital, and entrepreneurial skills. Variables such as the ability of governments to organize and mobilize national resources, home market protection, and industry structure have become increasingly important. As a first step in dealing with the new realities of industrial organization, the Unites States must have better information about how foreign industrial policies affect the shape and trajectory of our economy. We should try to identify which instruments of foreign industrial policy are most likely to produce benefits for their industry at our expense (for example, protecting their home market in order to gain benefits from learning-curve economies). Other policy tools (customized worker training, antitrust relief for R&D or production consortia) are more legitimate forms of government intervention and contain less of a zero-sum element.

We recommend that the United States work to strengthen and broaden the multilateral trading system. Reports of the GATT's death have been greatly exaggerated. Successful completion of the current agenda (better protection of intellectual property, strengthening discipline in agriculture, extending GATT coverage to services and trade-related investment, and improving dispute settlement and surveillance mechanisms) would help revitalize the multilateral trading system. The United States, however, has very little to bargain away during this round and should be wary of accepting limitations on the enforcement of its trade laws.

In addition, *we recommend that the United States begin to share the responsibilities of world trade.* The United States regularly takes a disproportionate share of world manufactured imports. In 1987, the United States accounted for 59 percent of developing-area manufactured exports to developed countries, as opposed to 29 percent for the European Community and 10 percent for Japan. One extreme example of this imbalance can be found in Hyundai's 1988 car exports. In that year, the United States imported 301,930, the European Community 20,097, and Japan 150.[2] A major objective of U.S. trade policy in the coming years should be to open foreign markets to the goods of *all* countries, rather than concentrating solely on U.S. export interests.

CONCLUSION

By necessity, trade policy must now be viewed as encompassing a broader set of issues: macroeconomic and structural factors that influence savings, investment, and domestic demand; exchange rate policies; competitiveness; and Third World debt. The current trade imbalances are unsustainable and threaten the stability of the world trading system. The United States must work to reduce these imbalances, but in a way that results in more, not less, trade and a higher standard of living for all participants. The United States must also recognize that the global balance and the composition of trade flows are as important as the overall level of world trade. In the final analysis, the United States cannot allow critical decisions about the evolution of its economy to be made by default, dictated by the narrow and chauvinistic trade and industrial policies of other countries.

NOTES

1. Architects of the postwar economic system wished to avoid the excesses of laissez-faire capitalism, however. Exchange rates were fixed, and all international economic agreements acknowledged the legitimacy of and need for domestic economic stabilization.

2. These 150 cars were a Special Olympic edition. In the first four months of 1989, Japan has only imported *seven* Hyundais.

BACKGROUND PAPER
by
Gary Clyde Hufbauer

To Clayton Yeutter
Energetic champion of free trade

Acknowledgments

Andreas Bender and Claudia Schmitz, both graduates of the Georgetown University MSFS Program, assisted in preparing this report. Helpful comments were given by Kimberly Elliott, Geza Feketekuty, Andrew Samet, and Jeffrey Schott, and by the members of the Twentieth Century Fund Task Force.

Chapter 1

Introduction: Two Challenges

During two terms in the White House, Ronald Reagan chalked up many economic accomplishments: U.S. unemployment fell to 5.4 percent in 1988, the lowest level since 1974; inflation dropped dramatically from 12.4 percent in 1980 to 4.1 percent in 1988; the top marginal tax rate was slashed from 70 percent to 33 percent; and U.S. manufacturing firms improved their productivity growth, from an average annual gain of 2.3 percent in the 1970s to an average annual gain of 3.9 percent in the 1980s.[1] There are, however, blemishes in this record.

The Problems

Cumulative U.S. budget deficits have been enormous; during President Reagan's eight years in office, the federal debt held by the public rose approximately $1,341 billion, from $709 billion to $2,050 billion.[2] U.S. merchandise trade deficits rose from $26 billion in 1980 to $127 billion in 1988, totaling $797 billion during the eight years of the Reagan administration. As a direct consequence of the trade deficits, the United States lost its position as the world's foremost creditor country and became the world's biggest debtor nation. Measured at book value, the U.S. position as a net creditor at the end of 1980 was $106 billion; at the end of 1988 its net debt reached about $533 billion.[3] The deterioration was about $639 billion.[4]

41

Consequently, George Bush faces two major and inter-related challenges in the arena of trade policy: First, he must shape U.S. macroeconomic policy to reduce the merchandise trade deficit; second, he must set the long-term goals and the short-term tactics of commercial policy.

Shrinking the Merchandise Trade Deficit

The first challenge is to reduce the merchandise trade deficit (referred to in this paper simply as the trade deficit).[5] As pollster Peter Hart observed: "I see my polls and listen to my respondents at focus groups, and the one thing that really bugs them, as relates to the economy, is trade."[6]

U.S. trade policy during the past eight years underscored this political fact: As long as the trade deficit looms large, trade policy will emphasize "solutions" that spotlight unfair practices abroad and erect barriers to the U.S. market.[7]

In the wake of mounting trade deficits, the Reagan administration's trade policy evolved through three stages. In the early 1980s, the administration deviated from its rhetorical proclamation of free trade in only two significant cases: the automobile Voluntary Restraint Agreements of mid-1981 and the Third Multifiber Agreement in December 1981. By the mid-1980s, however, the administration found itself on the defensive, confronted by mounting congressional criticism as the trade deficit grew. The administration answered its critics by imposing case-by-case protection, often justified as a principled response to foreign "unfair" trade practices.[8] Finally, in 1986, after James Baker had become secretary of the treasury, the administration launched a broad and aggressive policy designed to open a range of foreign markets (for example, Korean insurance and Japanese telecommunications) to U.S. exports. All in all, during the Reagan years, the share of U.S. imports subject to some form of restraint increased from about 12 percent in 1980 to about 23 percent in 1988; while the number of discrete actions designed to open foreign markets to U.S. exports rose from practically zero to several dozen.

Propelled by ever-growing trade deficits, Congress engaged in three years of debate and bargaining over the Omnibus Trade and Competitiveness Act of 1988. The result was a far less restrictive piece of legislation than seemed likely in 1987 or even early 1988. Nevertheless, the overall tone of the debate was "get tough on trade."[9]

Benefits usually result—for both trading partners—when barriers tumble down. Sometimes trade disputes are resolved quickly under the pressure of a statutory mandate. Nevertheless, excessive emphasis on this aspect of policy can lead to such bizarre outcomes as the U.S. government's assumption of a godfather role for a semiconductor agreement with Japan that hampered U.S. computer exports, and made the United States an antagonist with some of its closest allies.[10] Equally important, when senior U.S. officials spend most of their energy attacking specific foreign practices and defending particular U.S. producers, attention is distracted from the more general liberalization of trade and investment.

Economists have demonstrated that unfair practices abroad are not the main cause and not even a major cause of the U.S. merchandise trade deficit, and that U.S. restrictions on imports have been deployed far more extensively and far longer than can be justified for adjustment purposes.[11] Nevertheless, economic logic carries little weight in shaping the thrust of commercial policy. The political logic for a policy influenced by recrimination will endure as long as trade deficits remain huge.

On the basis of present U.S. macroeconomic policies, the trade deficit will shrink very slowly from its 1988 level of $127 billion. Based on present policies, projections indicate that the deficit will remain above $100 billion at least through 1991 (see Table 1.1). In order to restore a liberal thrust to trade policy, President Bush should deploy macroeconomic tools—especially exchange rates and fiscal policy—to correct the deficit at a more rapid pace. At the same time, he must also work with foreign leaders to maintain buoyancy in the world economy. A buoyant world economy will enable the United States to reduce its trade deficit by expanding its exports rather than shrinking its imports.

The virtues of a buoyant world economy should be self-evident. But history suggests otherwise. At this juncture of a prolonged economic recovery, when fears of inflation are mounting, central bankers could prematurely arrest the recovery by applying a stiff dose of tight money. President Bush, together with European and Japanese leaders, should agree to place more reliance on open markets and trade liberalization, and less reliance on high interest rates and slow growth, to arrest inflationary pressures. In addition, the industrial world should help revive the economies of developing countries that are burdened with debt, enabling them once again to become good export markets. The proposal by Secretary of the Treasury Nicholas Brady, announced in March 1989, offers a step in the right direction: private bank forgiveness of some debt of less developed countries, coupled with an accelerated pace of new lending by the International Monetary Fund, the World Bank, and the regional development banks.

Shaping Trade Policy

The second challenge facing President Bush is to chart the course of U.S. commercial policy. This involves both setting long-term goals and selecting short-term tactics. The broad goal for the year 2000 should be bold and ambitious: creating an area of free trade and investment that will encompass all members of the Organization for Economic Cooperation and Development (OECD).[12]

In its early stages, the OECD Free Trade and Investment

Area (FTIA) should set itself the task of coordinating the exchange-rate policies of its member nations with a view to reducing current account imbalances. This important task represents a modest extension of the goals already adopted by the seven Economic Summit nations: Canada, France, the Federal Republic of Germany, Italy, Japan, the United Kingdom, and the United States.

In its later stages, the OECD FTIA should attack all manner of trade and investment barriers. It should reach well beyond the elimination of tariffs and quotas and achieve such goals as harmonizing technical standards, providing uniform protection for intellectual property, creating open access to government procurement, enacting parallel corporate-takeover legislation, forging similar policies concerning competition, and creating comparable corporate tax systems.[13] These goals are bold, but they are not radical. To a large extent they have informally guided the working agenda of the OECD. But a dramatic statement by the Economic Summit nations of their long-term objectives is imperative to maintain momentum toward economic integration, to soften the edges of emerging regional trade blocs, to arrest the government-sponsored cartelization of trade, and to forestall the erection of new barriers against foreign investment. If President Bush accepts this advice and propounds the long-term goal of an OECD FTIA, what interim strategies can be devised to fulfill that goal? That question is difficult to answer because of the four competing and overlapping ideas that shape U.S. trade policy:[14]

1. The old standby is the multilateral approach embodied in the General Agreement on Tariffs and Trade (GATT). GATT doctrine emphasizes various "universal" obligations. Most important, each GATT member is obliged to trim its import barriers to allow every other GATT member to have the same access that the "most

favored nation" (MFN) enjoys (in other words, the MFN principle forbids preferences that constitute discrimination among GATT members). And each GATT member is obligated to accord "national treatment" to products imported from all other GATT members (foreign products, for example, should not be subject to discriminatory taxes or discriminatory health standards that are not imposed on domestic products).

2. Another idea that originated in the 1950s is the sectoral approach, whose proponents seek a balanced blend of trade management and trade liberalization carefully tailored to suit producer interests in both importing and exporting countries. This approach has been followed in successive multifiber agreements, the carbon steel arrangements, various U.S. and European automobile agreements with Japan, and the U.S.-Japan semiconductor agreements.

3. Yet another idea, explicit in U.S. trade policy since 1974, is retaliation in response to foreign "unfair" trade practices. Retaliation entails antidumping and countervailing duties designed to offset the "unfair" price advantages of foreign exporters and Section 301 reprisals designed to open foreign markets to U.S. goods and services.

4. Finally, there is the bilateral or plurilateral approach, whose proponents seek freer trade and investment between pairs of small groups of countries, for example, the enlargement and completion of the European Community, the U.S.-Canada Free Trade Agreement (FTA), and the Australia–New Zealand Closer Economic Relations (CER) Agreement. Such arrangements not only entail preferences in favor of partner countries (in other words, a departure from the MFN principle), but they also require partners to observe higher obligations than those imposed on GATT members to obey the rules of a "level playing field." (Broadly speaking, the "level

playing field" concept requires that each country accord equal treatment to all firms, whether they are based at home or abroad.)

To lay the groundwork for an OECD FTIA, it might seem that the best strategy is to emphasize first idea—multilateral liberalization across the board. Judging from the modest gains achieved in the Tokyo Round of Multilateral Trade Negotiations (1973–79) and the equally modest promise of the Uruguay Round (1986–89), however, sole reliance should not be placed on GATT talks. In fact, that approach is beginning to resemble King Arthur's quest for the Holy Grail.

Instead, different trade issues should be addressed in different contexts and country groupings—all based on the larger perspective of an OECD FTIA. For example, a retaliatory approach may provide the best weapon against entrenched barriers and unfair trade practices such as Japanese limits on foreign construction firms. Bilateral and trilateral approaches may work best for designing technical standards appropriate to pharmaceutical testing, high-definition televison, and value-added networks. Plurilateral approaches may work best for managing and even liberalizing trade in mature, slow-growing industries (for example, textiles and apparel, and carbon steel). A multilateral approach almost certainly works best for tariff reduction.

The many alternative negotiating forums do not, however, share the same probability of making real progress toward an OECD FTIA. In Chapter 4 it is argued that sector agreements are akin to the prince of darkness: very likely to be captured by producer groups and thus unlikely to promote trade liberalization. In Chapter 5 it is contended that retaliation is like the avenging angel: sometimes successful, sometimes destructive, but in any event not a force for broad reform. In Chapter 6 the conclusion is reached that free trade agreements are the white knights of the system: usually working for consumer interests and often leading to broader free trade and investment arrangements.

If the industrial nations are to achieve an OECD FTIA by the year 2000, the major building blocks will have to come from existing free trade arrangements—the European Community, the European Free Trade Association (EFTA), the U.S.-Canada Free Trade Agreement, and the Australia–New Zealand Agreement.

The Political Dimension

U.S. trade policy has never been pursued with single-minded attention to economic gain. Political goals have always been important. Indeed, the proponents of the Marshall Plan and the Bretton Woods institutions sought to spark the political renaissance of Europe and Japan against the threat of the Soviet Union. The commercial and financial institutions devised in those years did as much to forge the Western alliance as did the U.S. military agreements with NATO, Japan, Australia, and other allies.

The United States now faces the prospect of drifting farther apart from Western Europe both in military and in economic terms.[15] In military terms, the Intermediate Nuclear Force (INF) Treaty, coupled with growls from Washington about burden sharing and encouragement from Moscow about disarmament, points to a world of greater European self-reliance.[16] Meanwhile, disputes in the Western Alliance over replacing aging Lance missiles in West Germany and removing all short-range nuclear weapons from Europe have created new trans-Atlantic tensions.

In economic terms, the prospect of a unified market within the European Community in 1992 is raising concerns that European unity will be purchased in part at the expense of U.S. exports. Furthermore, Western Europe is rapidly expanding its trade and credits to the East, and progress toward a unified market within Western Europe could lead to dreams of a "common house" that would eventually embrace the states of Eastern Europe. At the very least, once the Europe 1992 exercise is complete, the European Community could pay more attention to absorbing Austria, Norway, and other EFTA nations than to its dealings with the United States. The strongest political argument for an OECD FTIA is that it may counterbalance the forces working to separate the United States and Western Europe.[17]

The second strongest political argument for an OECD FTIA is that it may dissipate the acrimony that increasingly distances the United States from Japan. If both countries can cooperate in working toward a larger economic goal that transcends their immediate concerns about rice exports, Honolulu real estate, and FSX fighter planes, then perhaps Japan and the United States can continue the postwar political alliance that has so successfully reshaped East Asia in a democratic, market-oriented direction.

The Omnibus Trade and Competitiveness Act of 1988

How should the 1988 act fit into the president's calculations? Briefly, it provides a window of opportunity for President Bush to put his stamp on trade policy. A short historical review helps explain why.

Between the Tariff of Abominations of 1828 and the Smoot-Hawley Tariff of 1930, a perennial issue on the congressional agenda was the level and the structure of tariff protection. Following the disastrous aftermath of the Smoot-Hawley Tariff, Congress delegated to the president much of its constitutional authority over U.S. trade policy.[18] This authorization was accomplished through enactment and renewal of the Reciprocal Trade Agreements Act of 1934, which gave the president considerable (but not unlimited) tariff-cutting authority.

In the context of the times, this division of responsibility between the White House and Capitol Hill proved to be satisfactory. During most of the period between the 1930s and the 1960s, U.S. industry dominated the world, the U.S. balance of payments consistently showed a surplus, successive presidents used trade policy as an instrument of foreign policy, and Congress avoided constituent pressures for protectionist relief.[19]

Eventually, however, U.S. economic dominance began to fade, new priorities emerged, and Congress began to reassert its constitutional role in making trade policy. The renewal of congressional involvement began with the Trade Expansion Act of 1962, which not only launched the Kennedy Round of GATT but also gave impetus to additional restrictions on textile and apparel trade, created a program of Trade Adjustment Assistance, and strengthened the Tariff Commission.[20] Twelve years later, the Trade Act of 1974 was passed. This act not only launched the Tokyo Round of GATT but also enlarged private access to U.S. statutes governing antidumping and countervailing duties and mandated that a minimum level of human rights would have to be observed before MFN status could be accorded to Soviet bloc countries (the Jackson-Vanik Amendment). The Trade Agreements Act of 1979 implemented the agreements reached in the Tokyo Round, strengthened various trade remedies, and provided an occasion for still tighter restraints on textile and apparel imports.

Each major trade act since the Trade Expansion Act of 1962 has thus given more detailed and precise directions to the president about the conduct of trade affairs, and each law has afforded greater rights of redress to U.S. firms that face competition from imports or foreign barriers to their exports.

The Omnibus Trade and Competitiveness Act of 1988 should be viewed as part of this trend. The 1988 act is a mammoth piece of legislation (eleven hundred pages) that provides detailed instructions to the president about a great many trade and nontrade matters and enlarges the rights of redress available to private industry and labor groups.[21] The objectives of the 1988 act are to improve market access for U.S. exporters, to reduce impediments that the United States imposes on its own exporters, and to make it easier for U.S. businesses to obtain relief from import competition. As an unspoken preamble, Congress has appealed to President Bush to accord international economic issues higher priority than they received from President Reagan.

The 1988 act provides carrots and sticks in pursuit of market access. The foremost carrot is the president's negotiating authority to conclude the Uruguay Round and bilateral trade negotiations. "Fast-track" procedures have been designed to ensure a quick congressional vote without amendment on any trade agreement submitted by the president before May 31, 1993.[22] These procedures give foreign nations a strong incentive to negotiate with the United States: If the president agrees to a deal, it will probably be enacted by Congress. That statement applies not only to the conclusion of the Uruguay Round, but also to the initial steps toward an OECD Free Trade and Investment Area.

Most of the sticks on behalf of market access work by increasing the likelihood that the U.S. government will take action against "unfair" foreign trade practices. Procedures and deadlines for applying Section 301, the statutory vehicle for responding to industry-specific complaints about foreign trade barriers, are stipulated in the act. In addition, "Super 301" was designed to combat systematic trade practices that restrict U.S. access to an entire national market.[23] The 1988 act reinforces U.S. support for agricultural export subsidies as long as other trading partners (especially the European Community) insist on subsidizing their own agricultural exports. The 1988 act also gives priority to more open telecommunications trade at a time when European and Japanese public telephone and data transmission systems are subject to strong buy-national pressures.

In order to reduce U.S. barriers to export expansion, the 1988 act substantially eases licensing requirements for the export of high-tech goods. It also takes some of the sting out of the Foreign Corrupt Practices Act of 1977: A U.S. business is no longer liable if it merely has "reason to know" that corruption exists in foreign transactions involving its goods or services.

Import relief was a third objective of the 1988 act. The laws governing antidumping and countervailing duties were expanded in procedural and definitional ways. Moreover, the 1988 act strengthened protection available (under Section 337) to owners of U.S. intellectual property. Violations are now easier to prove, and relief is easier to obtain. For example, under the 1988 act, U.S. companies no longer have to prove that they were injured in order to obtain protection from imported counterfeit goods.

Similarly, the national security provisions (Section 232) of the Trade Expansion Act of 1962 were tightened. The old law allowed the secretary of commerce one year to investigate and make a recommendation to the president, who faced no deadline in deciding whether to limit imports. The new law reduces the investigation period and imposes a deadline for presidential action.

Finally, the 1988 act provides an additional measure of relief for a domestic industry that can show the U.S. International Trade Commission that it has been harmed by fair imports. Relief can take the form of import restraints or adjustment assistance or both. The renewed Trade Adjustment Assistance (TAA) programs extend more generous training and other benefits to workers displaced by imports, and the 1988 act requires the president to seek a multilateral agreement covering the use of import fees to fund TAA.

The Omnibus Trade and Competitiveness Act of 1988 creates a broad mandate for presidential action. With the passage of this law, Congress temporarily took itself out of the trade legislation business. For the next few years, the president alone will formulate U.S. trade policy. Judging from recent legislative trends, this delegation of authority will not last indefinitely, but it should provide ample time for President Bush to put his stamp on U.S. trade policy.

Chapter 2

Macroeconomic Answers
to the Trade Deficit

The triple trajectories of growing federal debt, continuing merchandise trade deficits, and rising net external claims will almost certainly continue into the early 1990s.[1] The task facing the Bush administration is to decisively reverse the trade trajectory and to slow the ascent of federal debt and net external claims.

The most intractable problem is the federal budget deficit.[2] In fact, persistent merchandise trade deficits and rising external debt can primarily be traced to outsized federal budget deficits. If the United States follows the Gramm-Rudman-Hollings (GRH) targets (representing a zero budget deficit in 1993), additional federal debt of about $330 billion will be accumulated between 1989 and 1993; but because the U.S. economy is growing, the federal debt burden will decline from about 42 percent of Gross National Product (GNP) in 1988 to about 36 percent of GNP in 1993. By contrast, if the United States follows the Congressional Budget Office (CBO) baseline forecast, additional federal debt of about $730 billion will be accumulated, and debt held by the public will remain at about 41 percent of GNP through 1993.[3] It is clear that the White House will want to influence spending and tax policy to move closer to the GRH targets rather than the CBO forecasts.

What about the U.S. position as a net debtor in the international investment accounts? If U.S. merchandise deficits decline slowly from their 1988 level of $127 billion, as seems likely in the context of present economic policies, then U.S. current account deficits will continue to mount at more than $100 billion annually (see Table 1.1). The reason for gloom is that the net flow of international investment income, which was traditionally a source of strength in the U.S. balance of payments, has now turned negative owing to the rising external debt. Net payments of investment income to foreigners promise to become bigger in the years ahead, even as the merchandise trade balance gradually improves.

Each year the persistent U.S. current account deficit will require an equivalent amount of net capital inflows from abroad and thereby will add to the rising level of external debt. With annual current account deficits of over $100 billion, the U.S. net debtor position, measured at book values, could exceed $1,000 billion by January 1993 (see Table 1.1).[4]

The buildup of U.S. external debt would be more tolerable if it corresponded, dollar for dollar, to net additional real investment in the U.S. economy. There is scant evidence that this has happened. In the 1970s, when the United States was a net lender to foreign nations, gross fixed nonresidential investment within the United States averaged 10.8 percent of GNP. In the 1980s, when the United States became a net borrower, that figure was only 10.9 percent of GNP.[5]

These figures strongly indicate that foreign buyers bought existing U.S. assets from American sellers in the 1980s, while the economy on the whole increased its public and private consumption instead of creating new assets through higher real investment. In December 1993, when projected net external claims on the United States reach $1,100 billion, they will represent about 17.2 percent of U.S. GNP, or about 5.7 percent of total U.S. reproducible assets.[6] Suppose that President Bush adopts a goal of putting the U.S. balance of payments in shape so that the net external debt figure is gradually reduced to a target level of about 10 percent of nominal GNP during the ten-year period 1993-2003. What would that goal suggest in terms of tolerable trade deficits? The implications can be sketched.

In the year 2003, nominal GNP will reach approximately $13,200 billion.[7] Hence in that year a net external debt of $1,320 billion would represent an "acceptable" 10 percent of GNP. The year-to-year change in U.S. net external debt approximately equals the net inflow of foreign capital, which in turn equals the nation's current account deficit. Thus the implied permitted accumulation of current account deficits—the amount that would expand the net external debt from $1,100 billion in 1993 to $1,320 billion in 2003—would be about $220 billion over ten years. This would be consistent with an average U.S. current account deficit of about $20–30 billion per year, starting no later than 1993.[8]

By comparison, the projected current account deficit in 1993, under present economic policies, would be about $110 billion (see Table 1.1). An improvement in the current account of about $80 billion (say, reduced from $110 billion to $30 billion) would require a comparable reduction in the trade balance by the same amount—$80 billion—entailing a reduction from a projected deficit of about $80 billion to a balanced merchandise trade position in 1993.[9]

How can the trade balance be improved by $80 billion? In general, the tactics employed to achieve this goal can be grouped into two categories: microeconomic solutions, emphasizing better U.S. performance in particular markets and products, and macroeconomic solutions, emphasizing a more competitive exchange rate and lower federal deficits.

To provide a factual backdrop for examining the various solutions, Tables 2.1 and 2.2 give a breakdown of the U.S. trade deficit in terms of trading partners and product categories. Throughout the 1980s, the U.S. trade deficit worsened in every major area except the Organization of Petroleum Exporting Countries (OPEC) (see Table 2.1). Similarly, the trade deficit worsened in every product category except mineral fuels and miscellaneous items (see Table 2.2). The U.S. trade deficit deteriorated by about $101 billion between 1980 and 1988: The period began with a deficit of $26 billion and ended with a deficit of $127 billion (see Tables 2.3 and 1.1).

Microeconomic "Causes"

Proponents of popular explanations for past U.S. trade deficits emphasize injustices abroad and inadequacies at home. According to this line of thinking, the U.S. trade deficits of the 1980s can be attributed primarily to unfair foreign trade practices, lagging U.S. technology, and the poor quality of U.S. products. The solutions suggested by the proponents of this analysis call for a reversal of the underlying causes, country by country and industry by industry.

In fact, however, all the plausible microeconomic explanations can explain only a modest part of the burgeoning U.S. merchandise trade deficit. To be sure, ending foreign barriers should be the principal goal of U.S. trade negotiators, and the development of first-class technology and the production and the export of better products should be the major goals of U.S. corporate leaders. Over a period of ten or twenty years, these steps will prove decisive in shaping the *composition* of U.S. trade (more high-tech exports). Improvements in U.S. process and product technology can, moreover, better the *terms of trade* (the average price of exports divided by the average price of imports), and thereby significantly increase U.S. gains from participation in the international economy.

But even large strides toward ending foreign barriers and improving U.S. technology will do little to reduce the trade deficit. And unless effective macroeconomic steps are taken to curtail the deficit, U.S. negotiators will find it hard to make the concessions at the international bargaining table that are necessary to induce foreign nations to open their markets to U.S. goods and services. Certainly President Bush will find it difficult to marshal domestic political support for bold international initiatives such as the OECD FTIA; and, as long as extraordinarily large trade deficits persist, U.S. industrial corporations will find it hard to earn the profits necessary to finance new technology and better products. With these thoughts in mind, it is worth taking a close look at the popular microeconomic explanations of U.S. trade woes.

1. *Unfair Trade Practices Abroad.* Representative Richard A. Gephardt (D–Mo.) campaigned in the 1988 Democratic presidential primaries on the issue that unfair trade practices abroad play a leading role in the U.S. trade deficit. Echoing this theme, a major premise of the Omnibus Trade and Competitiveness Act of 1988 is based on the assertion that foreign barriers unjustly hamper U.S. exports. The examples are many: Korean barriers against Chrysler K cars; Japanese rice quotas, gasoline and soda-ash cartels, and supercomputer procurement policies; Brazilian restrictions on minicomputers; Western European restraints on California almonds and AT&T digital switches; and so on.[10] But analysis suggests that *rising* foreign trade barriers can explain only a small part of the total U.S. trade deficit.

Unfair trade practices are closely identified with non-tariff measures (NTMs)—such barriers as rigid inspection standards, agricultural quotas, government procurement policies based on buy-national commitments, and other measures. As Table 2.4 indicates, the United States erected more NTMs in the 1980s than did Western Europe or

Japan. "Hard-core" NTMs imposed by the United States rose from 11 percent of total U.S. imports in 1981 to 16 percent in 1986; the figures for the European Community were 12 percent and 15 percent; the figures for Japan were 25 percent in both years. By the "hard-core" standard, the Japanese market is by far the most protected. But among industrial countries the United States is the biggest "new sinner" in terms of piling *new* "hard-core" NTMs on those inherited from the 1970s.

A very rough estimate suggests that *new* "hard-core" NTMs imposed by other industrial countries in the 1980s may have cost the United States at most $6 billion of exports in 1986 and that *new* "hard-core" NTMs imposed by the United States in the 1980s may have reduced U.S. imports by about $17 billion in 1986.[11] In other words, it seems most unlikely that the U.S. trade balance was worsened by the imposition of NTMs during the 1980s; in crass mercantilistic terms, the United States "gave" better than it "got."

It is worth taking a glimpse at a better trading world largely free of such measures. After all, this is a major objective of the Uruguay Round and other trade negotiations. What would it mean for the United States if Western Europe, Japan, and other OECD nations completely removed their NTMs? The available data are not precise, but rough estimates suggest that U.S. exports might be stimulated to the extent of $20 billion annually by the elimination of all NTMs by the industrial countries (see Table 2.5). The corresponding estimates for the elimination of tariffs by the industrial countries suggest that U.S. exports might be expanded by $8 billion anually (see Table 2.6). These are not negligible figures, and the realization of such export gains is a major objective of U.S. trade negotiators.

The elimination by other industrial nations of their NTMs and tariffs might enlarge U.S. exports by $20–$30 billion annually. But it is most unlikely that other industrial nations will agree to unilateral liberalization. Following time-honored practice, they will insist on reciprocity—stipulating that U.S. NTMs and tariffs must be cut sufficiently to yield an equivalent expansion of U.S. imports. If past practice is repeated, trade will expand globally, but the U.S. trade deficit will be little affected by global trade liberalization.[12]

2. *Lagging U.S. Technology.* Many examples can be cited of industries in which the United States was once the world's technical leader and now has either lost leadership or must share its position with other nations. Affected sectors include advanced materials (high-performance ceramics, liquid crystals, and semiconductor materials), biotechnology, and robotics (see Table 2.7).[13] Reflecting this decline, the U.S. trade structure is decidedly less high-tech today than it was in 1970; the Federal Republic of Germany, France, and the United Kingdom have drawn even with the United States, and Japan is well ahead (see Table 2.8).

Although estimates are difficult to make, it is worth trying to figure out how much the U.S. trade balance worsened between 1980 and 1988 on account of the U.S. lag in high-tech products. For this exercise, we focus on high-tech manufactures, as classified by the U.S. Department of Commerce (see Table 2.2). We first consider exports and then imports. Underlying these calculations is an implicit assumption that savings and investment balances, both in the United States and abroad, would have adjusted to accommodate different export and import levels.

U.S. exports of high-tech manufactures compare very favorably with U.S. exports of non-high-tech manufactures. They also compare satisfactorily with world exports of high-tech manufactures. Between 1980 and 1987, U.S. exports of high-tech manufactures grew from $55 billion to

$84 billion; during that period, U.S. exports of other manufactures grew only from $106 billion to $116 billion. Consequently, U.S. exports of high-tech manufactures rose from 35 percent of all U.S. exports of manufactured goods to 42 percent. Moreover, during this period, U.S. exports of high-tech products grew almost as fast as world exports of comparable products.[14]

The real shortcomings in U.S. high-tech performance show up on the import side. U.S. imports of high-tech manufactures grew from $28 billion in 1980 to $84 billion in 1987, far faster than U.S. imports of non-high-tech manufactures. The comparison is between a 198 percent growth in imports and a 129 percent growth in imports.

One crude way to estimate the effect of lagging U.S. technology on the trade balance is to calculate the counterfactual growth of high-tech imports in the following manner. Suppose that, on account of macroeconomic forces, U.S. high-tech imports between 1980 and 1987 had grown as fast as non-high-tech imports, say, 129 percent. Then the counterfactual level of high-tech imports in 1987, assuming no technology lag, would be

> Counterfactual high-tech import level in billion dollars in 1987:
>
> $28 billion times (2.29) = $64 billion.

In fact, actual high-tech imports were $84 billion, or $20 billion higher than the calculated counterfactual impact of the U.S. level. The figure of $20 billion seems like a possible estimate of the impact of lagging technology on the U.S. trade balance.[15]

3. *Poor U.S. Products.* Another recurring complaint is the low quality of U.S. products and associated services such as delivery times and repair records. This complaint overlaps but is distinct from the criticism concerning lagging technology. The lagging technology criticism is usual-

ly focused on high-tech components and industrial processes; the poor quality complaint is focused on consumer durables. Frequently cited problems are poor industrial design and the mediocre workmanship of U.S. products.

Two products often singled out are automobiles and household appliances.[16] As Table 2.9 indicates, U.S. imports of these products soared in the 1980s, from $35 billion to $91 billion. In share terms, however, U.S. imports of road motor vehicles and household appliances as a percentage of total U.S. manufactured imports only rose from 28 percent in 1980 to about 30 percent in 1987. During that period, the percentage of imports of road motor vehicles and household appliances as a share of manufactures imported by the rest of the world remained constant at about 16 percent (see Table 2.9).

In other words, although U.S. imports of automobiles and appliances soared in dollar terms, they rose only slightly in share terms. Perhaps the explanation for the entire U.S. change in shares can be put under the general heading of poor quality. Based on this assumption, the quality problem might have worsened the U.S. trade balance in the 1980s by about $6 billion.

4. *Help from Petroleum Prices.* In the 1980s the microeconomic trade news was not all bad. The U.S. trade balance was substantially improved by a collapse of oil prices—from a Saudi Arabian benchmark price of about $29 a barrel in 1980 to a price of about $18 a barrel in 1987.[17] Correspondingly, the cost of U.S. mineral fuel imports dropped from $82 billion to $47 billion (see Table 2.2). It is reasonable to attribute the difference, about $35 billion, to microeconomic good fortune.

Summary of Microeconomic "Causes." The popular microeconomic explanations of U.S. export performance are summarized in Table 2.10. Paradoxically, this table suggests that all microeconomic events may have improved the trade balance in the 1980s, not worsened it. Quite possibly, the adverse impact of new foreign trade barriers, lagging technology, and the poor quality of U.S. products was more than offset by new U.S. nontariff measures and lower petroleum prices. In fact, the collective impact of microeconomic events may have improved the trade balance by as much as $20 billion.

Although no great reliance should be placed on this particular set of estimates, the exercise forcefully underlines the broad conclusion: The $101 billion deterioration in the trade balance between 1980 and 1988 cannot be explained by microeconomic events.

Macroeconomic Solutions

Weak U.S. trade performance in the 1980s must be attributed to powerful macroeconomic forces. Such forces can be divided into four broad categories:

- Dollar exchange rates
- Government deficits
- Private savings
- Growth in the rest of the world

If properly reversed, these forces will solve the U.S. trade deficit.[18] In the following analysis, the four macroeconomic forces are examined one at a time. In real life, of course, the forces interact with one another; for example, the level and the direction of the government deficit affect the exchange rate. For broad-brush purposes, however, no great harm will be done by ignoring the interactive aspects of the macroeconomy.

1. *Dollar Exchange Rates.* The exchange rate for the dollar acts as the "great price" that links the United States to the rest of the world. When the dollar rises in value

relative to foreign currencies, all U.S. goods and services become more expensive to foreign buyers, and all foreign goods and services become less expensive to American buyers. After a period of time, foreign buyers cut their purchases of U.S. products, American buyers increase their purchases of foreign products, and the U.S. trade balance worsens. Conversely, when the dollar falls, opposite price effects are felt throughout the world economy, and after a lag, the U.S. trade balance improves.[19]

Figure 2.1 portrays the giant roller coaster traced by the exchange value of the dollar in the 1980s. The dollar's strength between 1980 and 1985 allowed foreign producers to earn high profits while capturing markets from American producers, both in the United States and abroad. The dollar began its roller-coaster decline in February 1985. For many months foreign producers sacrificed profits in an attempt to hold market share, but U.S. producers are finally beginning to recapture lost ground.

Many estimates have been made of the impact of the value of the dollar on U.S. trade balance.[20] My own estimate, based on a rough appraisal of several macroeconomic models, is that in the late 1980s a one-index-point change in the Morgan Guaranty index of the nominal dollar exchange rate will exert a $3 billion impact on the U.S. trade balance after a lag of about four years. Between 1980 and 1985, the Morgan Guaranty index rose by 40 index points (see Table 2.11). If exchange rates had stayed at their 1985 level, this dollar appreciation could have been responsible for a deterioration in the trade balance by as much as $120 billion in 1988 compared with 1980. The fall of the dollar from 1985 to 1988, however, amounted to 43 index points. Eventually, this decline should improve the trade balance by about $129 billion; perhaps $110 billion of that benefit (about 85 percent of the total) had occurred by 1988. In the first half of 1989, however, the dollar rose by about 8 index points, and this appreciation, if maintained, will offset all the remaining prospective improvement in the trade balance.

What about future changes in exchange rates? A key policy issue facing the administration is how hard Treasury Secretary Nicholas Brady and Federal Reserve Chairman Alan Greenspan should work behind the scenes with other finance ministers and central bankers to prompt a gradual decline in the dollar.

Since the Louvre Accord of February 1987, the Group of Seven finance ministers have emphasized the virtues of exchange-rate stability—without quite defining the term.[21] In fact, from the standpoint of U.S. interests, there are good arguments to maintain the dollar at its present level. A strong dollar helps to avert inflationary pressures within the United States.[22] Moreover, cooperation in managing exchange rates is the most visible symbol of macroeconomic coordination among the OECD nations. In addition, foreign asset holders could well feel betrayed by a plunge in the dollar and consequently become more reluctant to finance the U.S. current account deficit without the compensation of much higher U.S. interest rates. Finally, foreign governments could view a substantial depreciation of the dollar as the alter ego of aggressive trade policy, and accordingly resist offering concessions in the Uruguay Round.

There is one compelling argument on the other side of the debate. A drop in the dollar would be the strongest action that the Bush administration could take to correct the trade deficit. A depreciation of the dollar by 17 index points in nominal terms from its index level of 105 in June 1989 (1980 = 100), in the context of a weak U.S. economy, would improve the trade position by up to $27 billion annually four years later, an improvement that would go a very long way toward correcting the trade deficit.[23]

On balance, President Bush has much to gain by taking concerted action on the dollar, well before the 1992 elections and well before the final push in the Uruguay Round. If the markets do not bring about a lower dollar, then the administration should continue deploying suitable policy measures to achieve that result.[24]

It is not enough to reduce the exchange value of the dollar in an orderly fashion. Two complementary policies are also essential.

First, the U.S. economy must be redirected from serving domestic markets into serving export markets (or replacing imports). In a full employment economy, this shift of emphasis would require the implementation of tighter monetary policy or more disciplined fiscal policy. However, as long as the economy is weak—growing at 2 percent or less per year—additional demand in the export sectors can be met by resources drawn from other sectors of the economy, without the necessity of a fiscal or monetary squeeze.

Second, the administration should seek international agreement that a central goal of macroeconomic coordination among G-7 countries will be the systematic reduction of current account imbalances.[25] Only after assurance has been given that huge trade deficits will not again be tolerated for long periods of time will business firms invest with confidence that the United States can serve foreign markets, and only the reasonable management of current account imbalances will lay a solid foundation for the achievement of international progress on difficult issues of trade policy.

2. *Government Deficits.* According to accounting definitions, a nation's current account deficit equals its public sector financial deficit (government spending minus government revenue) plus its private sector financial deficit (private investment minus private savings). Table 2.12 shows U.S. data for the various components of the accounting relationship involving private financial savings,

public deficits, and external balances during the period 1981–88. The accounting framework provides a useful starting point for analyzing the connection between government deficits and trade deficits. But it does not demonstrate that a reduced government deficit will necessarily lead, dollar for dollar, to a smaller trade deficit. In fact, the link between U.S. budget deficits and U.S. trade deficits is not nearly as strong as the phrase "twin deficits" would suggest. Why is the connection weaker than the phrase? The reason is simple: A smaller government deficit might prompt a reduction in private financial savings rather than a fall in the trade deficit.[26]

Between 1984 and 1988, for example, the United Kingdom shrank its fiscal deficit from 3.9 percent of Gross Domestic Product (GDP) to 0.8 percent of GDP, yet the current account balance worsened from a surplus of 0.6 percent of GDP to a deficit of 1.3 percent of GDP. During that period of fiscal austerity, British private financial savings withered.[27] Conversely, during a recession, the government deficit might well worsen, but private savings could increase. For example, during the U.S. recession of 1974–75, the federal deficit rose from $12 billion to $69 billion, but the U.S. current account surplus rose from $2 billion to $18 billion. The counterpart of the combined $73 billion increase in the federal deficit and the external surplus was a $73 billion increase in private sector financial savings.

Despite these contrary examples, most models of the U.S. economy demonstrate that changes in government finances do affect the external balance.[28] A rough estimate suggests that, in the 1980s, the U.S. trade deficit worsens by approximately $25 billion for an increase in the fiscal deficit by 1 percent of GNP, after a period of three to five years.[29] Based on this estimate, the worsening of the budget deficit from an average level of $57 billion in fiscal 1979 and fiscal 1980 (2.2 percent of GNP) to an average level of $153 billion in fiscal 1987 and fiscal 1988 (3.2 percent of GNP) accounts for a deterioration in the trade balance by about $25 billion.

What about the future? According to the CBO baseline forecast (which assumes the maintenance of present revenue and spending policies) the unified budget deficit will gradually decline to about $135 billion in fiscal 1993, or about 2.1 percent of GNP.[30] The budget improvement of about 1.1 percent of GNP between 1988 and 1993 should translate into an improvement in the trade balance of about $28 billion. Many economists have urged the White House and Congress to reduce the budget deficit more quickly by raising taxes. In the 1988 presidential campaign, George Bush was crystal clear about the prospects for a tax hike:[31]

> May 31, 1988: "I've pledged no tax increase, and I'm going to stay with it. Yes, there's a period. No time limit."

> June 24, 1988: "I promise you, I'll not raise taxes as a first, second, or last resort."

> August 19, 1988 (Republican convention): "Congress will push me to raise taxes, and I'll say no, and they'll push me again, and I'll say to them, 'Read my lips: No new taxes!'"

> October 13, 1988 (Bush-Dukakis debate): "And so what I want to do is keep this expansion going. I don't want to kill it off by a tax increase."

> November 21, 1988 (after the election): "I am not going to change my view as to how we get this deficit down."

Financial shocks, political realities, and the mere passage of time will eventually render these campaign promises and post-election pronouncements obsolete. Meanwhile, it is realistic to expect two developments. First, Congress may come to accept the principle that any *new* programs, such as long-term health care, must be financed by *new* revenues allocated to specific programs.[32] The acceptance of that principle would at least prevent the worsening of the deficit (by comparison to the CBO baseline forecasts) through new spending programs.

Second, in the annual combat over the GRH targets, the president may accept some new, broadly defined "user" fees (for example, higher taxes on alcohol and tobacco to help pay for existing federal health and drug-abuse programs or new gasoline taxes to help fund the Strategic Energy Reserve and the construction of roads and bridges), and assorted loophole closing measures, all in exchange for congressional spending cuts.[33] The painful process of budget bargaining could perhaps squeeze $15 billion annually out of the deficit, or as much as $60 billion in four years.

My projections assume that, through some combination of forces, including mandated sequestration of budget outlays under the GRH legislation, the federal deficit will be cut to $70 billion in 1993 as opposed to the CBO baseline forecast of $135 billion. The budget improvement, about 1 percent of GNP, would in turn improve the trade position by about $25 billion.

3. *Private Savings.* In the 1980s private savings rates in the United States were poor both by historical standards and by comparison with other countries (see Table 2.13). It is not clear why U.S. household savings fell so much, but several hypotheses have been offered:

- Confidence in the economy rose, and there was less concern about saving for the proverbial "rainy day."
- Rising stock exchange and real estate prices created the same gains in private wealth that more private savings would have achieved, and so householders questioned the efficacy of saving.
- Improvements in Social Security, Medicare, and

private health and pension plans eroded householders' incentives to save.

• Despite the cut in marginal tax rates and despite high real interest rates, the tax structure still favors current consumption.

• High real interest rates enabled many pension plans to meet their financial targets with lower savings levels.

• Fear of nuclear war prompted some households to enjoy life now, rather than save for the future.

Whatever its origins, the impoverished U.S. savings rate is regrettable for two main reasons. First, and most important, it erodes U.S. competitiveness on a world scale. Domestic savings rates largely determine domestic investment rates (see Figure 2.2), and domestic investment in manufacturing largely decides the rate of productivity growth (see Figure 2.3). The low level of U.S. savings is thus a major cause for lagging U.S. competitiveness vis-a-vis its industrial rivals. Second, the meager savings rate harms the trade balance. The lower the rate of private savings, the greater the trade deficit for any given amount of federal deficit and private investment. In the 1980s a decline in the household savings rate of 1 percent of GNP probably caused a $25 billion increase in the trade deficit. Thus, the decline in personal savings from an average of 4.9 percent of GNP in 1979–80 to an average of 2.6 percent of GNP in 1987–88 was possibly responsible for a $58 billion worsening of the trade deficit.[34]

Because the U.S. household savings rate in 1987–88 was near its postwar low, it seems reasonable to expect that a favorable upward trend in savings will occur during the Bush administration—perhaps for reasons that have little to do with economic policy.[35] For example, American consumers may be sated with autos, boats, and TVs; glasnost has diminished their fear of nuclear war; and an end to the forty-year boom in housing prices could prompt householders to increase their personal savings rather than rely on ever-appreciating real estate prices to create the family nest egg.[36] Indeed, in the first half of 1989, personal savings jumped to 3.9 percent of GNP.

The projections in Table 2.13 assume that the personal savings rate will reach 4 percent of GNP by 1993. The realization of this assumption would improve the trade balance by $35 billion.

4. *Growth in the Rest of the World.* Some part of the rising U.S. trade deficit during the 1980s can be attributed to slow growth in other OECD nations and the collapsing fortunes of developing countries. In the 1970s the OECD nations other than the United States (ROECD) grew at an average rate of 3.7 percent, while the United States grew at an average rate of 2.8 percent. In the 1980s ROECD growth fell to 2.8 percent.[37] The slowdown in ROECD growth by about 0.9 percent per year between the 1970s and the 1980s contributed to increasing the U.S. trade deficit by about $9 billion annually.[38]

The troubles of the developing world are well known. The most significant cases from the standpoint of U.S. exports concern the developing countries of the Western Hemisphere. Between 1980 and 1987 U.S. exports to the countries in this hemisphere dropped from $39 billion to $35 billion. If the Western Hemisphere had not experienced the debt crisis and deteriorating terms of trade, U.S. exports in 1987 might have been $12 billion higher.[39]

Perhaps the arithmetic of growth can be turned around in the late 1980s and early 1990s. If the rest of the world economy grows faster, the United States will have an easier time curtailing its own trade deficit. In economic terms, foreign markets will be more receptive to U.S. goods. In political terms, there will be less resistance by foreign central banks to a lower dollar and less resistance by foreign trade ministers to concessions designed to open overseas markets to U.S. products.

Fortunately, a good part of the pro-growth battle has been won in Japan. Spurred by fiscal relaxation and an investment boom, Japanese growth picked up from 2.5 percent in 1986 to 5.7 percent in 1988. Even in Western Europe there are signs of faster growth. The key player is the Federal Republic of Germany. In 1988, West German growth rose to about 3.4 percent, from 2.3 percent in 1986. The forecasts in Table 2.13 assume that the combined forces of self-interest and diplomacy (including the growth stimulation of the Europe 1992 process) will cause ROECD growth to increase by 1 percent per year in the late 1980s and 1990s over the growth recorded in the early and mid-1980s.

The industrial nations must also promote more robust growth in the developing world. The Asian nations of the Pacific can take care of themselves. The major problems are found in the indebted countries of Latin America and Africa, and their difficulties raise issues that go well beyond the scope of this paper. Nevertheless, U.S. export interests are very clear, especially in the Western Hemisphere.

Both the debt crisis and weak U.S. exports to this region have been exacerbated by transfers of net resources in the wrong direction—from the countries of the Western Hemisphere to international financial institutions and private banks. A plausible program for reversing the transfer from Latin America would involve a step-up in World Bank and International Monetary Fund lending of about $10 billion per year and an increase in new commercial bank lending of about $10 billion per year.[40] If such a program were adopted, the developing countries of the Western Hemisphere could increase their imports by $20 billion annually, and U.S. exports to the region might increase by about $8 billion per year. A program of this nature makes good political and economic sense, and the tally in Table 2.13 reflects the export consequences.

Summary of Macroeconomic Solutions. The origins of the burgeoning trade deficit are summarized in the second panel of Table 2.10. All the decisive forces had a macroeconomic origin. The strong dollar and the rising federal budget deficit perhaps explain $50–60 billion of the rise in the trade deficit. Equally important is the collapse of household savings, which accounted for $50–60 billion of the total. Slow growth in the rest of the world may have accounted for $20 billion. Just as the origins of the merchandise trade deficit were located in the macroeconomy, so will the cure be found there.[41]

Table 2.14 suggests one possible clue to future events. Improvement in the federal deficit and private savings, as a percent of GNP, coupled with June 1989 exchange rates, may well improve the trade balance by $50–60 billion over the next four years. Three additional policies would virtually eliminate the trade deficit by 1993: a fall in the nominal exchange value of the dollar from its June 1989 level by approximately 17 percent over the next two years, a decrease in the federal deficit to a level of about $70 billion by fiscal 1993, and modestly higher growth both in the ROECD nations and in the indebted nations of the Western Hemisphere.

Chapter 3

The Uruguay Round

The General Agreement on Tariffs and Trade is not a free trade organization.[1] Rather, it is a system of managed mercantilism for the trading of goods. GATT's disciplines consist of four principal elements:[2]

- The most-favored-nation clause of Article 1
- The national treatment clause of Article 2
- A commitment to use "transparent" rather than "opaque" trade policy instruments
- A commitment to liberalize trade barriers in the context of reciprocal negotiations

Under the auspices of GATT, there have been seven rounds of multilateral trade negotiations designed to implement these disciplines. The seven GATT rounds have succeeded in reducing tariff levels substantially—in the case of the United States, from an average of roughly 13 percent on dutiable imports in 1946 to an average of less than 5 percent by 1988.[3] Low average tariff rates have also been achieved in Canada, Western Europe, and Japan. By the early 1960s Western Europe and Japan had largely abolished exchange controls and quantitative trade restrictions.

Trade liberalization ushered in a tremendous growth of world commerce particularly between the 1950s and the 1970s. In turn, the expansion of commerce propelled a remarkable spurt of economic growth. Between 1950 and 1970, the ratio of exports to GNP for the industrial countries rose from 7.4 percent to 10.4 percent, and the GNPs of industrial countries grew at an average rate of 4.4 percent.[4]

As far as trade matters are concerned, the world of the 1980s is far from free. Many quantitative restrictions (QRs) remain, especially on agricultural products, and new QRs are being created to "safeguard" ailing industries. Moreover, as the outer shroud of "transparent" tariff barriers has been cut, other administrative measures have been exposed—not only QRs but also government procurement, subsidies, and product standards. The GATT system has made little headway in reducing these assorted, often "opaque," nontariff measures (NTMs) for several reasons:

- Governments prefer to deal with the difficult adjustment problems of sunset industries by retarding imports rather than by taking costly and painful measures to close old plants and retrain the work force.
- Governments are eager to boost high-tech industries by using whatever means are available, including trade restrictions.
- Nontariff measures often entail government measures that fall outside the purview of trade ministers, for example, bank regulation and pharmaceutical standards.
- The GATT membership is now so large (ninety-seven countries plus nine observers) and includes countries in such disparate economic circumstances that it is difficult to reach agreement on a balanced package for the liberalization of NTMs.
- In the past, members have often ignored the GATT dispute settlement machinery. Without a working mechanism to resolve disputes, commitments to reduce NTMs are meaningless.

Not surprisingly, in the face of these difficulties, the momentum of growth in world trade has slowed. One good index of the contribution that trade policy makes to the expansion of world trade is the difference between the rate of growth of exports and the rate of growth of output.[5] As Table 3.1 shows, the difference between the annual growth of manufacturing exports and the annual growth of manufacturing output has dwindled from decade to decade— from 3 percent in the 1960s to 1.5 percent in the 1980s. In the case of agriculture, the growth of trade exceeded the growth of output by margins of 1.5 to 2 percent in the 1960s and 1970s, but the two growth rates were practically the same in the 1980s. The good news, in terms of this index, should not be overlooked: in 1988, merchandise export growth, at 8.5 percent, exceeded output growth by 3.5 percentage points. This can probably be be attributed to the buoyant world economy, and the fact that no major new trade restraints were imposed in 1987 or 1988.

The decadal comparisons between world trade and world output growth comport with common sense: The effect of the cumulative trade expansion from the abolition of exchange controls in the 1950s and the first four GATT rounds—Geneva (1947), Annecy (1948), Torquay (1950), and Geneva (1956)—was greater than the combined effect of the trade expansion from the Dillon Round (1960–61) and the Kennedy Round (1964–67), which in turn was greater than the effect of the Tokyo Round (1973–79). In fact, the Tokyo Round made far more progress in codifying acceptable mercantilist practices than in slashing trade barriers. As a practical matter, the Tokyo Round probably expanded world exports by only 1 to 2 percent.[6]

This brief history explains the characterization of further GATT talks as a quest for the holy grail. Certainly the objective is worthy, and certainly the quest should be undertaken. But no one should expect the ultimate goal— trade liberalization in a world of level playing fields—to

be reached by this means alone. Let us examine the progress to date in the Uruguay Round.

After much difficulty and delay, the eighth round of
GATT trade negotiations was launched in 1986 in Punta
del Este, Uruguay. The Uruguay Round is widely regarded as critical to the viability of GATT,[7] and U.S. leadership is critical to the success of the round. In these talks,
the United States has espoused four key objectives:

- *Agriculture:* Eliminate agricultural subsidies, and
achieve much freer agricultural trade by the early years
of the twenty-first century.
- *Services and intellectual property:* Establish a
framework that precludes discrimination against foreign
firms and that protects trademarks, patents, and
copyrights in world markets.
- *NTMs:* Achieve a level playing field so that all firms
get a fair shot at world markets, especially in high-tech
products.
- *GATT machinery:* Ensure that GATT dispute panels
operate according to reasonable timetables and that
GATT surveillance mechanisms spotlight restrictive
practices.

On the first three points, the United States is at odds
with its key trading partners. The European Community
does not want to dismantle its high-subsidy, high-
protectionist Common Agriculture Policy (CAP). Many
countries (but not those of Western Europe and Japan) fear
the strength of U.S. financial, data-processing, consulting,
and accounting firms. Developing countries do not want
to strengthen the intellectual property rights of industrial
nations, and most countries refuse to abandon a legion of
NTMs that protect high-tech and low-tech sectors alike.
Only on the question of GATT machinery is there
widespread agreement that mechanisms for the resolution

of disputes and for surveillance should be significantly improved.

Despite these difficulties, the talks conducted under the Uruguay Round are well under way. They are conducted in three main groups: the Surveillance Body on Standstill and Rollback, the Negotiations on Goods (comprised of fourteen negotiating groups), and the Negotiations on Services. The structure of the talks is portrayed in Figure 3.1.

The midterm review, held in Montreal, Canada, December 5–9, 1988, made progress in a number of areas but ended with a stalemate on agriculture and intellectual property. Consequently, the members agreed to reconvene in Geneva, Switzerland, in April 1989, to hammer out agreement on a single text. The complete report of the Trade Negotiations Committee (TNC) was issued after the April meeting. (Bearing the code Restricted MTN. TNC11, 21 April 1989, it is referred to in the discussion that follows as the Montreal Report.) In the fall of 1989, prodded by Arthur Dunkel, Director-General of GATT, the members agreed to the following timetable: all substantive proposals to be tabled by December 1989; negotiations to be largely concluded by July 1990; legal text to be drafted by December 1990. Following the April 1989 review, here is the state of play.[8]

Surveillance Body on Standstill and Rollback

The Surveillance Body is the least effective of the negotiating groups in the Uruguay Round. As a price for participating in the Uruguay Round, the developing countries insisted that the industrial countries dismantle existing measures that are inconsistent with GATT (the rollback concept) and not engage in new inconsistent measures (the standstill concept). The Surveillance Body was created to oversee those obligations.

In the course of its deliberations, the Surveillance Body

has come to distinguish between "GATT-inconsistent" measures, namely, practices that a panel has pronounced to be in contravention of GATT; and measures "not consistent with GATT," namely, practices that experts have pronounced to violate the spirit of GATT but may be consistent with the letter of GATT. Not surprisingly, the United States and some other industrial countries contend that the Surveillance Body should focus on "GATT-inconsistent measures," whereas (rhetorically at least) India and some other developing countries argue that the mandate of the Surveillance Body also extends to measures "not consistent with GATT."

In any event, most of the notifications to the Surveillance Body concern the application of the standstill obligation to GATT-inconsistent measures. Most complaints have been filed by certain industrial countries against other industrial countries. For example, the European Community prevailed in 1987 in a finding by a GATT panel that the U.S.-Japan semiconductor agreement wrongly escalated semiconductor prices in Western Europe, and the European Community has now asked the Surveillance Body to examine Japanese compliance with the finding. The United States has objected to Canadian dairy quotas and subsidies for peas and new subsidies by the European Community for rice and quotas for apples. Despite these instances, it is not readily apparent that the Surveillance Body has so far improved compliance with GATT obligations. Hence the Montreal Report both reaffirmed the standstill commitment and emphasized the need for action on GATT-inconsistent measures.

The practical effect of the rollback obligation remains obscure. Although existing trade measures that are not consistent with the spirit of GATT run into the hundreds, offending countries can usually find something in the extensive legal practice of GATT to justify their "gray area" measures;[9] and accusing countries run the risk of endangering their prospects for obtaining concessions on other issues by bringing complaints. For these reasons, the Surveillance Body has had precious little rollback work. An exception occurred in March 1988 when the European Community tabled an offer to rollback approximately ninety residual quantitative restrictions maintained by member states. The offer was subject to the tabling of other offers; so far, the United States, Japan, and other countries have not responded.[10] In any event, the Montreal Report reaffirmed the rollback commitment and called for a substantive evaluation of progress in July 1989.

Negotiations on Goods

At center stage in the Uruguay Round is the group called the Negotiations on Goods. At the top of the group is the Supervisory Group. The fourteen working groups underneath can be divided into four broad clusters: Trade Barriers, Sectors, the GATT System, and New Issues. The fourteen separate negotiations cover the core of GATT concerns: world merchandise trade of about $2,500 billion annually and potential liberalization that could result in an expansion of exports by hundreds of billions of dollars.

1. *Tariffs.* In previous GATT rounds the average tariff levels of the major industrial countries were reduced to low levels, generally under 6 percent, but the average tariff levels of most developing countries remain at quite high levels, generally more than 30 percent.[11]

The tariff section of the Montreal Report called for substantive negotiations to begin in July 1989 and highlighted mutual concessions that should be sought. Two major concessions that developing countries can make in the round are to reduce their very high tariff levels and to "bind" their tariff rates in GATT.[12] Two major concessions that industrial countries can make are to flatten the peaks in their tariff profiles (the residual high tariffs that protect "sensitive" products such as apparel, footwear, ceramics, and seasonal fruits and vegetables) and to diminish the extent of tariff escalation (the practice of affording greater protection to processed goods than to raw materials).[13] In essence, the Montreal Report called for tariff concessions that will be at least as ambitious as those achieved in the Tokyo Round.

The export expansion resulting from the complete elimination of tariffs imposed by the industrial countries would be about 5 percent of their affected imports, or about $70 billion annually (see Table 2.6). Comparable estimates are not available for trade on the part of the developing countries, but a conservative guess is that a 50 percent cut in their tariffs might expand world trade by $70 billion.[14] Both estimates constitute large magnitudes, and the realization of a partial amount might well be the most significant contribution of the round. At Montreal, the participants agreed to a general target of at least 30 percent tariff reductions by all GATT members.

In June 1988 seven countries tabled a tariff-cutting formula that was designed to reduce high tariffs proportionately more than low tariffs.[15] The modalities of bargaining about tariffs were not resolved at Montreal, but the United States is not enthusiastic about formula cuts. The remaining high U.S. tariffs protect sensitive products such as orange juice and footwear, and the United States wants to negotiate those tariffs individually in a request-and-offer context that would also involve NTMs.[16] In this context the United States could secure reciprocal concessions best tailored to mute the political reaction of powerful domestic industries. However, the United States now stands practically isolated in its resistance to formula tariff cuts.

2. *Nontariff Measures.* Nontariff barriers are the main protective shield imposed by many countries. Quantitative restraints are especially prominent; other NTMs include restrictive technical standards, buy-national preferences, and labeling requirements. NTMs may well limit the im-

ports of industrial countries by approximately $260 billion annually (see Table 2.5).

Industrial countries do not have a monopoly on NTMs. Although data on developing countries are not available, casual observation reveals that their NTMs are at least as restrictive as those of industrial countries. The elimination of NTMs by developing countries might well expand their imports by at least $70 billion annually.[17] Now that the successful newly industrializing countries (NICs) in Asia have become huge players in world trade, the United States has accorded priority to gaining access to their markets, many of which are protected by long-standing NTMs. For both industrial and developing countries, there is a great deal at stake in the NTM battle: perhaps $330 billion of lost trade.

In November 1987 Australia tabled a proposal that would have all forms of government assistance to an industry or a product, including NTMs, measured by a single parameter called the effective rate of assistance (ERA). In July 1988 fifteen countries responded by suggesting that a formula approach rather than request-and-offer bargaining should be applied to the reduction of NTMs.

Although superior in principle to simpler methods, a common measure, coupled with formula reductions, would be difficult to apply in the Uruguay Round. The necessary spadework to assemble a complete inventory of NTMs and to measure ERAs remains to be done. This requires the cooperation of GATT members, and despite the efforts of the GATT Secretariat, many countries simply refuse to acknowledge their own gray-area trade restrictions.[18]

Moreover, the United States takes the position that a code approach can be applied to only a few NTMs such as preshipment inspection and rules of origin.[19] The United States wants to negotiate most NTMs on a request-and-offer basis for the simple reason that NTMs are its biggest bargaining chip. This is shown in Table 2.5, which

contains estimates of the potential expansion of imports—
approximately $55 billion in the case of NTMs imposed
by the United States.

The Montreal Report did not resolve the negotiating
modalities—both request-and-offer and formula methods
were recognized as possible approaches. In the report,
however, the members did assert that no country should
receive concessions in exchange for meeting its rollback
commitments; and they suggested that, when an NTM
cannot be eliminated, the country that imposed the NTM
should consider transforming it into a tariff.

3. *Natural Resource Products*. Trade in products composed of natural resources, excluding energy, amounts to
about $130 billion annually; in addition, trade in energy
products amounts to about $270 billion.[20] Import restric-
tions on products composed of natural resources are
generally low; moreover, many of those products are supplied by multinational enterprises that provide a political
bulwark against trade restrictions.

From the standpoint of producing countries, the major
problem of the natural resource sector is weak prices. But
price-stabilizing and price-raising schemes, such as the ill-
fated Tin Agreement and the almost bankrupt International Cocoa Organization, are not subjects for the
Uruguay Round.

From the standpoint of the United States, the main concern is centered on the use of subsidized natural resources
to make upstream products, for example, cheap petroleum
or natural gas supplied by a state enterprise used by
private firms to make ammonia fertilizer, or low stumpage
fees applied to logs taken from a state forest used by
private firms to make cut lumber.

With such fundamental disagreement about the essence
of the problem, this group has experienced difficulty in
transcending listless discussion. The Montreal Report

called for "effective negotiations" as soon as possible, starting with the exchange of data concerning trade and barriers by March 1989. The report noted that some progress has been made on fisheries, forestry, and nonferrous metals.

4. *Textiles and Apparel.* Textiles and apparel products together account for about $160 billion of trade, about 9 percent of the world exports of manufactured goods.[21] As a result of two decades of Multifiber Agreements (MFAs), however, trade in textiles and apparel is highly restricted. With free trade, imports of textiles and apparel by the industrial countries could easily increase by $50 billion annually.[22]

In general, bilateral quotas imposed under MFAs enable industrial countries to restrict the exports of developing countries, but the MFA system also protects weaker LDC exporters (for example, Colombia and Kenya) against stronger exporters (for example, Taiwan and Hong Kong). The system also enables efficient producers in countries such as Hong Kong to earn large "quota rents."[23] There are few multinational enterprises operating in this industry, and thus there is no effective producers' lobby for freer trade.[24] Almost any liberalization would leave some powerful group of producers worse off than they are under the MFA system, and that prospect alone may be enough to sustain the system indefinitely. The most recent Multifiber Agreement, signed in 1986, will be reviewed in 1991, when it seems almost certain that the MFA will be renewed for another five years.

Undaunted by practical realities, Pakistan has submitted a proposal that envisages the dismantling of the MFA system in four phases. First, restrictions imposed on the imports of apparel based on the criterion of low prices would be abolished, together with all restrictions on nonapparel textiles. Second, import restrictions on apparel textiles would be relaxed. Third, the maintenance of remaining restrictions would require the approval of the Textile Surveillance Body (TSB).[25] And fourth, all MFA restrictions would be removed. Similar proposals have been made by other developing countries, but, needless to say, most industrial countries and many developing countries consider such proposals to be almost insupportable.

At the April meeting, the members agreed broadly to discuss "the phasing out of restrictions under the Multifiber Agreement and other restrictions on textiles and clothing not consistent with GATT rules and disciplines." This language contains at least the glimmer of a commitment to eliminate MFA restrictions by the year 2000.

5. *Tropical Products.* This is one of the few negotiating groups that reached agreement in time for the Montreal review. Tropical products are generally not produced in industrial countries, and the exceptions (for example, sugar, rice, and tobacco) are either defined or cross-referenced as agricultural products.[26] The annual trade volume of items covered solely by the tropical products group is about $40 billion.[27] Tariffs imposed by the industrial countries on selectively defined tropical products are low, and most taxation takes the form of domestic consumption taxes. Hence it was easy to reach agreement on improvements in access to markets.

In October 1987 the European Community offered to reduce or eliminate tariffs, QRs, and consumption taxes on a broad range of tropical products amounting to about $9.5 billion of trade. In January 1988 Japan offered to improve its regime on about one-third of the tropical products that it imports, which amount to about $3.3 billion. For a while, the United States tried to link progress in tropical products with progress in agriculture in order to mobilize the support of the developing countries against European agricultural practices. This ploy was abandoned in September 1988 when the United States agreed to reduce barriers on 130 tropical products involving imports of about $500 million.[28]

As a result of these concessions made by the industrial countries, it was possible to reap a very satisfactory "early harvest" on tropical products at the December review. The Montreal Report calls for the elimination of duties on unprocessed products, the elimination or the substantial reduction of duties on semiprocessed and processed products (with a view to reducing the escalation of tariffs), and the reduction of all nontariff measures. At the April meeting in Geneva, early implementation was agreed to on liberalization measures covering some $20 billion of tropical products trade.

6. *Agricultural Products.* The group on agricultural products is the key to the entire Uruguay Round.[29] World trade in agricultural products, about $330 billion, is highly distorted by subsidies and is constrained by barriers.[30] Ever since the Great Depression, the United States and Western Europe have deployed various output-limiting plans, price-support schemes, import restraints, and export subsidies in an effort to maintain farm income. Strictly in budget terms, these programs cost the United States about $27 billion and the European Community about $22 billion in 1986. In overall economic terms, the consumer costs of agricultural protection in industrial countries runs to about $220 billion annually.[31] If restrictions did not exist, trade volume would be much larger; for example, world exports of coarse grains might increase by 30 percent, beef and lamb exports might increase by 235 percent, and sugar exports might increase by 60 percent.[32] World agricultural trade is probably diminished by at least $100 billion annually because of agricultural restraints.[33]

In the early 1950s, in order to harmonize GATT with their interventionist ways, Western Europe and the United

States introduced amendments to GATT Article 11 that permit quantitative restrictions on agricultural imports. In 1955 the industrial powers carved agriculture out of the Article 16 disciplines on export subsidies. In the 1960s Japan joined forces with the other industrial countries in limiting agricultural imports. By the 1980s very few countries could claim free trade in agriculture, and seven rounds of GATT negotiations have made little progress in arresting or dismantling restrictive practices.[34]

In 1985 the Cairns Group was formed by countries whose exports suffer most from the agricultural programs of the industrial nations.[35] (The Cairns Group is named after the Australian resort town, on the Queensland coast, where the inaugural meeting was held.) In 1986 the Cairns Group squarely dealt with the question of agriculture in the Punta del Este declaration.

In July 1987 the United States tabled its own far-reaching proposal to address agricultural issues: All programs and restrictions should be included in a common measure of public support to agriculture, the public subsidy equivalent (PSE), and all PSEs should be eliminated according to a phased schedule over ten years (that is, by the year 2000). A similar schedule would be worked out to eliminate import restrictions. After ten years, the only support programs still allowed would be direct farm income payments unconnected to production and marketing. In other words, remaining farm-support measures would be decoupled from farm-output levels. All countries would agree on a clear distinction between boosting farm income and raising farm prices. The decoupling concept is intended to ensure that world markets are no longer burdened by mountains of grain and lakes of milk.[36]

When the Cairns Group presented its own proposal in October 1987, after the U.S. proposal was made, it seemed almost conservative. The group proposed standstills on both subsidies and on restrictions against market access and commitments to reduce the large agricultural stocks held by the United States and the European Community. It called for an agreement to use a common yardstick such as the PSE to eliminate public support and restrictions on market access over an unspecified period of time.

In July 1988 the Cairns Group followed up its proposal by suggesting: (1) an immediate freeze on trade-distorting agricultural subsidies and 10 percent reductions during 1989 and 1990 (developing countries would be exempted from this stage); (2) ministerial agreement in Montreal on the rate of PSE reductions in subsequent years; and (3) negotiations beginning in 1989 on the full liberalization of agricultural trade in the long run.[37]

Shortly before the Montreal meeting, the United States embraced the more flexible proposals of the Cairns Group (including a two-year freeze on support, subsidies, and protective measures) as a way of increasing pressure on the European Community. The United States also suggested that all QRs be converted into tariffs (a proposal already adopted by Japan on beef and citrus) as a way of improving the transparency of trade barriers and building pressure for their removal. In addition, the United States and other countries agreed to endorse the aggregate measurement of support (AMS) rather than the PSE as the common guidepost for farm trade policies. The difference is that the AMS excludes measures that do not distort trade, for example, publicly funded agricultural research and import-inspection systems. Finally, President Reagan himself acknowledged that the goal of ending all agricultural subsidies by the year 2000 was unrealistic.[38]

The European Community meanwhile called for reform at a slow pace involving a limited range of products such as cereals, sugar, and dairy products.[39] In essence, the European Community offered to trade better access to Western European markets and some discipline on Western European export subsidies in exchange for the maintenance of world prices.

The outcome of all this economic diplomacy was that,

before Montreal, common ground existed between the proposals tabled by the United States and the Cairns Group. But the European Community remained most reluctant to cut agricultural protection especially while negotiating to form the Europe of 1992.[40] Japan, most concerned about protecting its rice farmers, stayed on the sidelines.[41]

The outcome in Montreal was a stalemate. The European Community would not accept the long-term goal of eliminating all trade-distorting subsidies (the zero option). The United States would not accept the short-term goal of a freeze, in isolation from other measures, lest it prematurely sheath the retaliatory weapons contained in the Trade Act of 1988. At one point, the acrimony became so intense that the European Community and the United States talked about pulling agriculture out of the Uruguay Round and settling their agricultural differences bilaterally. The Cairns Group rejected this suggestion and threatened to walk away from the entire round. The members finally agreed to reconvene in Geneva, Switzerland, in April 1989, when new negotiators entered the arena: Carla Hills for the United States and Frans Andriessen for the European Community. The report issued in April 1989 divides the agricultural problem into long-term elements, short-term elements, and arrangements on sanitary and phytosanitary regulations.

Under the heading of long-term elements, the members agreed that their ultimate objective is "to provide for substantial progressive reductions in agricultural support and protection sustained over an agreed period of time." This language reflects a concession to the European Community.

The long-term objective will be reached through commitments reached within the AMS framework—a concession to the United States and the Cairns Group. Commitments within the AMS framework are supposed to bring agricultural practice into conformity with GATT rules, for example, by eliminating QRs in favor of tariffs, by making income-support measures more responsive to international price signals, by curtailing export subsidies, and by eliminating export restrictions.

Under the heading of short-term elements, the members agreed on a qualified standstill for their domestic protection and export support levels. They also stated an intention to reduce support and protection levels for 1990, either within the AMS framework or by taking specific policy measures. Undertakings in respect of this commitment are to be announced by October 1989.

Finally, the April report invites GATT members to harmonize their sanitary and phytosanitary regulations (regulations that deal with such issues as hormones in beef and pesticide residuals on lettuce) over the long term.

7. *Safeguards.* Under GATT Article 19, if imports cause or threaten serious harm to a domestic industry, a member can suspend its GATT obligations and take defined "safeguard" (also known as escape-clause) actions to protect that industry. Over the years, the industrial countries have increasingly resorted to safeguard measures that violate the precepts of Article 19 and fall outside the disciplines of GATT: Their safeguards have been selective rather than multilateral; they have been semipermanent rather than degressive; and they have used quantitative restraints rather than tariffs.[42]

After much dispute and negotiation, the Group on Safeguards has come to accept the notion that safeguards can be selective rather than multilateral. In other respects the original spirit of GATT Article 19 still finds support. Thus, the Group on Safeguards has discussed the possible elements of a code that would cover all safeguards and require safeguard actions to be degressive, time limited, and accompanied by restructuring measures.[43]

A safeguards code would principally benefit developing

countries. In trade negotiations something is never given for nothing. One of the more promising deals now being considered involves willingness on the part of industrial countries to discipline their recourse to safeguards (Article 19) coupled with willingness on the part of developing countries to discipline their recourse to trade restraints for balance-of-payment reasons (Article 18), the so-called Article 18 for Article 19 trade-off. In any event, the Montreal Report did not extend much beyond generalities. The chairman of the group has been authorized to prepare a draft text, which was circulated in June 1989 as a basis for negotiations.

8. *Subsidies and Countervailing Duties.* GATT Article 6 authorizes members to levy countervailing duties when they face imports that are subsidized by the government of the exporting country, and Article 16 prohibits export subsidies on nonagricultural products. The Tokyo Round Code on Subsidies and Countervailing Measures listed prohibited subsidies and specified procedures for levying countervailing duties. But the code also sanctioned a great many incentive practices, and it allowed wide latitude for the national determination of countervailing measures.

Almost no one is happy with the resulting obligations and prohibitions. Many countries are aggrieved at the frequency and the variety of countervailing measures imposed against their exports, and others are aggrieved at widespread subsidy practices that flourish under GATT loopholes. Not surprisingly, those views correspond to whether a country is an initiator or a target of countervailing duties. As Table 3.2 shows, between 1980 and 1985 the United States was by far the largest user of countervailing duties, followed by Chile, Australia, Canada, and the European Community. The targets were widespread, and it is fair to say that, apart from the United States and

Chile, most countries view the issue from the perspective of a target rather than an initiator.

Thus, the Group on Subsidies and Countervailing Measures is deeply divided between those members that want to focus attention on limiting countervailing duties and those members, like the United States, that believe that the fundamental problem is the weak and inadequate GATT discipline on subsidy practices. The Montreal Report set forth a negotiating agenda that is broad enough to include all the contentious topics: the identification of prohibited subsidies both by means of a "red list" and by enumerated criteria, the identification of nonprohibited but actionable subsidies, criteria for taking remedial action, the range of permitted remedies, and the identification of nonactionable subsidies both by means of a "green list" and enumerated criteria.

9. *GATT Articles.* The task of the Group on GATT Articles is to suggest improvements in the legislative framework, namely, the General Agreement itself. This is an impossibly broad brief, and, as committees do in such circumstances, the group has concentrated its attention on resolving problems of immediate interest to its members. The Group on GATT Articles has taken up two issues of broad significance.

One is the ease of forming a customs union or a free trade area and the limited nature of the obligations imposed on contracting parties entering into such arrangements by GATT Article 24. The most effective free trade areas (notably the European Community) can produce large trade diversion effects, and from a bureaucratic standpoint, they pose a serious threat to the continued vitality of GATT itself. One outcome of this review may be the insistence that free trade areas create substantially more trade with outside countries than they divert from those countries.

The other problem addressed by the Group on GATT

Articles is Article 18(B), which permits developing countries almost unlimited access to trade restraints when they
invoke a balance-of-payments rationale. In the past, GATT
reviews of balance-of-payments controls have been perfunc-
tory; some developing countries have maintained balance-
of-payments controls for a decade or longer. There is the
possibility that developing countries will discipline their
Article 18(B) rights if developed countries discipline their
Article 19 rights—the Article 18 for Article 19 trade-off
mentioned earlier. For example, developing countries may
accept that balance-of-payments controls must not be of
indefinite duration and must not be maintained on a
product-specific basis; instead, they must be imposed across
the board for a limited time or not at all. As a constructive step, in June 1989, South Korea agreed to discuss how
it might eliminate its Article 18 controls.

In any event, the Montreal Report on this group was particularly bland and merely ended up with a call for clari-
ty and precision in defining the issues.

10. *Multilateral Trade Negotiation Agreements.* The
Group on Multilateral Trade Negotiation (MTN)
Agreements is concerned with the various Tokyo Round
codes.[44] This covers a great deal of ground and often
overlaps the other negotiating groups. The three codes that
the group has concentrated on are the Agreement on
Technical Barriers to Trade (Standards), the Agreement
on Import Licensing, and the Agreement on Antidumping. The Montreal Report made few specific proposals and
merely urged vigorous negotiations among group
members.

A good example of the group's work is the review of the
Antidumping Code. Antidumping duties are a mainstay
of retaliation against unfair trade: Between 1980 and 1985,
the United States initiated 280 cases, Australia initiated
393 cases, Canada initiated 219 cases, and the European

Community initiated 254 cases.[45] Even Mexico has become an avid proponent of antidumping actions. In fact, antidumping measures could easily become the growth channel of protection in the 1990s.[46]

Nevertheless, the United States has proposed adding features to the GATT Antidumping Code similar to those in its own expansive Omnibus Trade and Competitiveness Act of 1988, for example, measures dealing with repeat dumping. As a result, the European Community, which often suffers from U.S. antidumping actions, has proposed various measures to discipline the imposition of antidumping duties. On the other hand, the European Community has suggested rules against "screwdriver plants"—barebones local assembly plants often used by Japanese companies to obtain access to Western European markets and thereby avoid antidumping duties on final products. Japan, which is the most common target of U.S. and Western European antidumping actions, has been most energetic in proposing rules that would limit antidumping actions.

Bargaining among the United States, Japan, and the European Community may lead to modifications of the Antidumping Code. If so, a key goal should be to circumscribe the broad and potentially protective reach of national antidumping statutes.

11. *Functioning of the GATT System.* The Functioning of the GATT System (FOGS) Group has three main briefs: to strengthen the role of the GATT Secretariat in reviewing the policies of member countries; to coordinate work among GATT, the International Monetary Fund (IMF), and the World Bank; and to consolidate the leadership role of major trading countries.

There is broad support among the members for the GATT Secretariat to undertake a more active surveillance of trade policies. One proposal accepted at Montreal is that

GATT should review trade policies more thoroughly than it has in the past—once every two years for Canada, the European Community, Japan, and the United States; once every four years for the next sixteen largest trading countries; once every six years for most other countries; and a longer interval for least-developed countries. This proposal is known as the Trade Policy Review Mechanism (TPRM). The TPRM reports will be published with the expectation that over time they will serve to mobilize elite opinion against restrictive trade measures.

The practical dimensions of maintaining coordination among GATT, the IMF, and the World Bank are far from clear. One difficulty stems from the fact that the GATT Secretariat is small and poorly financed compared with the IMF and the World Bank. That means that it has historically served as a note taker for GATT members rather than as a proponent of policies—a very different role from that of the IMF and World Bank staffs. Even with this mismatch in staff roles, the three organizations can cooperate in the preparation of TPRM reports.[47]

More controversial is the question of GATT management. In terms of governance, there is a wide spectrum of international institutions. At one end of the spectrum are institutions in which the United States, the European Community, and Japan collectively exercise decisive influence. All the international financial institutions (the IMF, the World Bank, and others) belong to this group. At the other end of the spectrum are institutions in which one-nation/one-vote power gives developing countries a decisive influence, for example, the United Nations General Assembly and the United Nations Conference on Trade and Development (UNCTAD). Even though GATT's ninety-seven members follow a formal one-member/one-vote rule, the organization does not actually belong to the second group, because decisions are not taken by majority vote. Instead, decisions are taken by consensus and conciliation, and deference is accorded to the views of the major trading nations.

The United States and perhaps other major nations would like to move GATT closer to the first group of institutions. A proposal has been tabled to create a small Committee of Ministers that would meet two or three times a year. This committee would operate something like the IMF Interim Committee, which manages the affairs of the International Monetary Fund. Not surprisingly, developing countries fear that the Committee of Ministers would turn into a "rich countries' club" that would exercise undue influence on GATT. Consequently, there are tensions concerning the existence and the composition of this committee.

12. *Dispute Settlement.* Many criticisms have been leveled at GATT dispute procedures, but apart from agriculture, most disputes are settled in an orderly fashion;[48] for example, U.S. complaints about the restrictive implications of the practices of the Canadian Foreign Investment Review Agency were adjudicated and resolved by a GATT panel in 1984.

GATT dispute settlement procedures face two problems. The first is soluble; the second is not. The soluble problem concerns the fact that procedures are cumbersome and discretionary, which allows the defending country to drag out disputes and block the adoption of panel reports. The Group on Dispute Settlement has therefore recommended reforms to deal with the speed of verdicts, the selection of panelists, panel procedures, and the creation of a permanent arbitration body in Geneva, Switzerland. Canada and twelve other countries worked out a timetable of procedures that was accepted at Montreal. The new regime for the settlement of disputes will apply to complaints filed after May 1, 1989. An early landmark case will decide the legitimacy of U.S. sanctions imposed against imports from

Brazil (covering $39 million of trade) arising from a Section 301 complaint over the inadequacy of Brazilian protection for pharmaceutical patents.

The new dispute settlement regime envisages consultations between the parties for a period of sixty days (thirty days in "urgent" cases, including cases involving perishable products); thereafter the GATT director-general will appoint panel members if the parties have not agreed on the names of panelists within twenty days; panel reports will be issued within six months (three months in "urgent" cases). One reform that was not accepted is to deny the parties to a dispute the power to block the adoption of panel reports by the Council of Ministers (the so-called minus two proposal); at Montreal, industrial and developing countries alike overwhelmingly decided to retain their blocking powers.[49]

The insoluble problem in GATT dispute settlement procedures is the absence of an enforcement mechanism, beyond moral suasion. If a contracting party refuses to honor the verdict of GATT, the only recourse open to the aggrieved member is its right to retaliate. This right has little value if the complainant is small and the offender is big—a problem common to all international institutions and one that GATT is unlikely to solve.[50]

13. *Trade-Related Intellectual Property Rights.* Intellectual property rights include patents, trademarks, and copyrights—intellectual property that is registered with a national agency and is protected against infringement within the country's borders.[51] Trade-related intellectual property rights (TRIPs) are those rights that affect imports or exports of merchandise.

The piracy of patents and copyrights is particularly damaging to high-tech firms, such as Merck and Microsoft, and music stars, such as Michael Jackson; whereas trademark protection is vital for fashion firms, such as

Dunhill, Calvin Klein, and Gucci. U.S. business firms claim to have lost $24 billion of sales in 1986 alone from the infringement of intellectual property.[52] A British expert claims that counterfeit goods represent 3 percent to 6 percent of world trade.[53]

The first initiative of the Group on TRIPs was to commission the World Intellectual Property Organization (WIPO) to study the current state of national laws and international cooperation to those rights. The studies, which were completed in 1987, cleared the decks for bargaining within the TRIPs Group.

The protection of intellectual property within a country requires three measures: national legislation that defines the scope of property rights, an administrative capability to register rights, and a judicial mechanism to adjudicate disputes. The international protection of intellectual property rights requires that countries close their borders to pirated or counterfeit goods irrespective of whether the offense harms domestic or foreign holders of the rights.[54]

The European Community tabled sweeping proposals that emphasize minimum standards of protection for intellectual property rights, national treatment in granting intellectual property rights, and international measures to stop trade in pirated and counterfeit goods.[55] The proposals were generally endorsed by the United States, Japan, and other industrial countries. However, the United States believes that the European Community proposals do not provide for adequate enforcement measures. Meanwhile, the developing countries have resisted the designation of any minimum level of protection for intellectual property.

Broad agreement will be easiest to reach on a code against international commerce in pirated and counterfeit goods—goods that purloin a patent, a copyright, or a trademark. But the intellectual property community will not settle on a piracy/counterfeit code alone. It also wants agreement on minimum standards of protection for intellectual property used within national boundaries.

In the end, the Montreal Review was stalemated, and questions concerning intellectual property were deferred to the April meeting. India argued that GATT was an improper forum for considering issues relating to intellectual property other than counterfeit goods and contended that all other questions pertaining to intellectual property should be addressed solely in WIPO. The industrial countries are willing to accept WIPO model laws as the basis of standards governing intellectual property, but they long ago abandoned hope that WIPO could enforce such standards.[56]

The Indian position was reinforced by the acute resistance expressed by many developing countries against the protection of patents bearing on pharmaceuticals and food-related chemicals (for example, pesticides). This is a volatile issue in poor countries where drug and food costs are of vital political concern. Twenty years ago, medicines in India were among the most expensive in the world. Today, they are among the cheapest—in part owing to the absence of patent protection. But patent protection is also a vital issue to business: U.S. pharmaceutical companies estimate that they lose $200 million in sales to Brazil alone on account of the infringement of patents.[57]

At the April meeting, a text prepared by GATT Director-General Arthur Dunkel was accepted. This text papers over the key disputes (for example, the question of the proper role for WIPO, and the weight to be accorded the conflicting claims of economic growth, the promotion of research and development, and the diffusion of technology). All in all, progress on TRIPs in the Uruguay Round promises to be slow and difficult.

In addition to the Uruguay Round negotiations, the United States is putting bilateral pressure on a multitude of countries that allow counterfeiting and piracy—for example, Brazil, China, Hong Kong, India, Mexico, Singapore, South Korea, Taiwan, and Thailand. The statutory vehicles invoked by the United States are Section 337, used against pirated and counterfeit merchandise that makes its way to the United States,[58] and Section 301, used against "priority countries" that systematically infringe U.S. intellectual property rights in their home markets or in shipments to third countries. Many of the target countries are susceptible to U.S. pressure, and it is likely that the United States will achieve its minimum objectives, if not in the TRIPs Group, then through bilateral settlements.[59]

14. *Trade-Related Investment Measures.* The issue of trade-related investment measures (TRIMs) was included at the last minute in the Uruguay Round declaration at the insistence of the United States.[60] Almost half of U.S. merchandise trade is conducted between affiliated firms,[61] and this fact has prompted U.S. concern about "performance standards," for example, requirements that multinational firms meet certain local content or export standards as a condition of doing business or receiving incentives in the host country. This is not an idle fear: approximately half of recent U.S. investments in developing countries entailed local content requirements or minimum export requirements.[62] Some observers view those requirements and the incentives associated with them as backdoor subsidies that distort the location of investments and the sourcing of components.

Since the Punta del Este declaration, however, U.S. interest in TRIMs has flagged. On the one hand, most U.S. companies are willing to accept TRIMs in exchange for incentives granted by host countries, and so there is no great enthusiasm within the business community for pursuing this issue. On the other hand, if strident members of Congress have their way, the United States would become a practitioner of performance standards, for example, requiring Japanese firms that invest in the United States to conduct a certain amount of research and development in the United States or to use U.S. auto parts in assembling vehicles.

Because U.S. interest is flagging, negotiations are proceeding at a desultory pace. The OECD countries want to establish some international rules, but they have not come to an agreement on the details. The United States and Japan, for example, would like to define TRIMs broadly, whereas the Western Europeans want to focus on local content and export performance requirements. The developing countries, led by Brazil and India, energetically oppose any GATT coverage of TRIMs. They strongly believe that performance requirements are a valid means of managing foreign investment, and they argue that the whole subject falls squarely within the scope of sovereign domestic policy. The third camp includes the newly industrializing countries, especially the Association of Southeast Asian nations (ASEAN). These countries are reluctant to relinquish control over their investment policies, but as a concession they are willing to consider some sort of broad framework to govern TRIMs.

Very little was accomplished on TRIMs at Montreal. Indeed, the report on this subject is a model of empty prose. To help revive the TRIMs talks, the influential Business Round Table has formed a special committee, chaired by Lillian Fernandez of Pfizer, to monitor progress and spur negotiations. In July 1989, both the United States and Switzerland tabled proposals listing numerous "red light" prohibitions against offensive TRIMs.

Meanwhile, the United States has pursued investment issues bilaterally, using both sticks and carrots. The sticks are Section 301 of the Trade Act of 1974 (amended in 1984 to include performance requirements) and Section 307 of the Trade and Tariff Act of 1984 (covering export-performance requirements). The carrots are a series of bilateral investment treaties (BITs) and the U.S.-Mexico Trade and Investment Framework.[63] These BITs and other agreements assert the right of establishment and the right to national treatment, and they contain weak provisions limiting harmful performance standards.

Negotiations on Services

The Negotiations on Services cover a large number of internationally traded business services, excluding, however, international payments of investment income (dividends and interest). Total world exports of business services (sometimes referred to as nonfactor services) were about $500 billion in 1987, about 20 percent of world exports of goods. Included in this category are travel and transportation, royalties and intellectual property fees, fees for financial services, communication, construction engineering, and film rentals.[64]

The inclusion of services in the Uruguay Round was the major bone of contention between the United States and the developing countries. The developing countries opposed the application of GATT principles or any principles of trade liberalization to services. Because of this inauspicious beginning, the Services Group spent 1987 reviewing facts and discussing concepts.

U.S. negotiating objectives called for a broad framework agreement that ensures the transparency of barriers, the progressive liberalization of barriers, the right of national treatment, and nondiscrimination according to the most-favored-nation principle. In a significant U.S. triumph, these principles were generally accepted in the Montreal Report. At the insistence of developing countries (especially Brazil and India), however, there is escape-hatch language for safeguards and exceptions, and, at the insistence of the European Community, there is a reference to "market access," a phrase that is widely perceived as an opening for the reciprocal treatment of Western European banks in the U.S. and Japanese markets.

The current task is to translate agreement on framework principles into a reasonably tough framework code and to negotiate individual sector agreements consistent with the framework principles. Advocates for open trade in financial services have largely inspired the negotiations on services. A notable and dedicated proponent is Harry Freeman of American Express. It remains to be seen whether other service sectors, such as air transport and shipping, will now work to slow the momentum for liberalization. At the April meeting, it was agreed to examine the implications of the broad framework principles for six "sample" sectors: telecommunications, construction, transport, tourism, financial services and professional services (such as law and accountancy).

It is too early to say how negotiations will proceed, but Australia has suggested a procedure for sector agreements based on exceptions: Every country would list those national regulations that do not comply with the framework rules for a sector. Mutual bargaining would then lead to the progressive removal of regulations from the exceptions list. The Australian proposal is based on arrangements in the Australia–New Zealand Closer Economic Relations Agreement.

Developing countries are still wary of the effort on services. To begin with, they regard the escape-hatch language as a means to avoid liberalizing their nurtured home industries such as banking and insurance. In addition, India and Mexico, speaking for many developing nations, have argued for freer access to the markets of industrial countries for services in which the developing countries command a comparative advantage, for example, construction work.[65] The Montreal Report included, among the negotiating topics, "cross border movement of factors of production where such movement is essential to suppliers." This formulation could be just broad enough to satisfy the developing countries and just narrow enough to avoid the explosive specter of roving bands of migrant workers arriving in Los Angeles or London.

Realistic Goals for the Uruguay Round

As this sketch suggests, the list of issues before GATT is extensive. The United States, as the chief proponent of the Uruguay Round, wants new rules on a wide variety of subjects. Most other nations simply want peace: They want to avoid U.S. countervailing duties, antidumping duties, and Section 301 reprisals. Given this stance, the Uruguay Round will accomplish far less than its champions hope. But the talks should not collapse, nor should they conclude with a meaningless affirmation of the status quo.

Serious negotiations began in 1989, once the presidents and prime ministers who will conclude the bargain took office in the United States, Canada, Japan, and the key countries of Western Europe. Two central questions thus face the Bush administration: What is the size of a minimum acceptable deal? What is the United States prepared to pay for that deal?

1. *The Size of the Deal.* It is too much to hope that GATT can seriously attack the deep structure of protection behind national borders. A discordant group of ninety-seven members cannot hope to agree on such difficult issues as appropriate investment incentives, patent practices, and electronic standards. Some observers urge that the way out of the impasse is through the extension of the Tokyo Round code approach.[66] Under the code approach any GATT member can join a code provided that it is willing to subscribe to the code obligations. In principle, then, the code approach enables the design of tough disciplines and associated privileges that will be open to all. In practice, there are two major problems with the code approach.[67]

- There is a strong tendency for the code to reaffirm the status quo because "spoiler" countries insist on participating in code negotiations only to weaken the disciplines that are included in the final text.
- Code negotiations lack the broad-based political support that enables the serious sacrifices that in turn get at deep-seated structural protection.

These inherent obstacles point to a single conclusion: The United States should abandon the cherished assumption that the Uruguay Round can effectively deal with a broad range of behind-the-border barriers. To be sure, such barriers are important. A very few can be addressed in the Uruguay Round; more can be examined on a bilateral basis; and many await the establishment of the OECD Free Trade and Investment Area.

The Uruguay Round should concentrate on the historic mission of GATT talks: to eradicate border barriers. This mission will provide an ample challenge for the most ambitious statesman. As Figure 3.1 suggests, old-fashioned border barriers may restrain $400–500 billion of merchandise trade alone. A frontal attack on these barriers could surely expand commerce by $150 billion, or by 6 percent of world trade—several times the gains reaped in the Tokyo Round. President Bush should announce such a goal; in fact, "$150 billion or fight" would not be a bad slogan for Bush to put to the Economic Summit powers in 1990.

According to this conception, the bottom line for the Uruguay Round would look like this:

- *Tariffs:* Reduce industrial-country tariffs to a low average level (eventually, say, 3 percent). Put an upper limit on developing-country tariffs (say, 25 percent). Bind all tariff commitments.
- *Nontariff measures:* Convert quantitative restrictions into tariffs or auctioned quotas. Leave the hard bargain-

ing over other NTMs to bilateral talks and free trade areas.

• *Textiles and apparel* and other sectoral arrangements: Over time bring these arrangements into conformity with a new Safeguards Code, emphasizing the conversion of QRs to tariffs and the progressive reduction of all barriers.

• *Agriculture:* Convert QRs to tariffs and gradually eliminate trade-distorting subsidies according to the AMS standard.

• *Safeguards:* Commit to time-limited, degressive, nondiscriminatory safeguards, preferably using tariffs rather than QRs.

• *Intellectual property:* Exclude counterfeit and pirated imports from industrial-country markets and devise a code of minimum protection standards to be signed by like-minded nations.

• *Services:* Seek a broad framework agreement embodying a standstill on new barriers, a commitment to national treatment, acceptance of the right of establishment, a commitment to transparent measures, and an endorsement of the principle of nondiscrimination. Agree on a few sector arrangements consistent with those principles (for example, financial services, shipping, air transport). Leave negotiations on other sectors to free trade areas and bilateral talks.

• *GATT machinery:* Improve dispute-settlement procedures and the GATT Secretariat surveillance of trade policies; establish a small Council of Ministers to manage GATT affairs.

As soon as this basic package has been put together— stripped of complex details and acrimonious talks about such subjects as high-definition television standards, government procurement of telecommunications equipment, and the propriety of irrigation programs—there will be no reason to delay the conclusion of the Uruguay Round beyond its 1990 timetable. To be sure, the European Community will still be in the midst of its own negotiations for 1992, but there is no practical way that the Uruguay Round can "leapfrog" the unification of Western Europe.[68] The European Community, the United States, and Japan should attempt to resolve issues raised by the Europe 1992 process on a bilateral and a plurilateral basis.

2. *U.S. Concessions.* Even a basic package will not be cheap. The United States will have to make concessions to reduce border barriers and to attack selected behind-the-border measures. The main U.S. concessions will be centered on sectoral reform: liberalizing highly protected agricultural products such as sugar, dairy, and meat and accepting the principle of eventual free trade in protected manufactures such as carbon steel and textiles and apparel.

The United States will also be asked to discipline the application of its future safeguard actions to obtain a larger adjustment component and a smaller protective component, and it will be pressured to accept some international review of its countervailing duty, antidumping duty, and Section 301 determinations, perhaps along the lines of the dispute-settlement procedures contained in the U.S.-Canada Free Trade Agreement.

From a mercantilist perspective, these are large concessions. The Bush administration will need considerable skill to negotiate such concessions with Congress. Any concessions, however, will be matched, dollar for dollar, by U.S. gains—improved access to foreign agricultural markets, much better protection of intellectual property, and far lower developing-country tariffs. The deal is worth doing.

Chapter 4

Sector Arrangements:
Prince of Darkness

A decade ago French leaders advocated "organized free trade" as a recipe for addressing the difficult problems of troubled industries. At the time, the phrase was derided as an oxymoron. But organized free trade expressed in sector agreements has increasingly become the policy style not only of the European Community and Japan but also of the United States. The coverage of goods and services is impressive: starting with selected agricultural products and airline and shipping services in the 1950s; reaching textiles and apparel in the early 1960s; extending to carbon steel in the late 1960s; encompassing automobiles and semiconductors in the 1970s and 1980s; covering military trade among NATO countries for three decades; and now threatening to encroach on civilian aircraft and financial services.

Two notable sector agreements paved the way for broad free trade arrangements, the European Coal and Steel Community of the 1950s and the U.S.-Canada Automobile Agreement of the 1960s. But unlike most sector agreements, the objective of these agreements was to eliminate trade barriers.

Most sector agreements have been concluded for quite different reasons:

• The industry in question is plagued by low demand growth or excess capacity. This is especially true of agriculture, shipping services, and carbon steel.
• Comparative advantage is often shifting to countries that have recently acquired a good command of production technology. This has been true of textiles and apparel, automobiles, and carbon steel. In the 1960s the newcomer was Japan; in the 1980s the newcomers have been Korea, Taiwan, and Brazil.
• Some important countries manage their domestic markets and foreign trade, prompting other countries to follow suit in defense of their own national industries. Airline services, military goods, and semiconductors are examples.

Most sector agreements have yielded two major results. First, they have served to mute competition by allocating market shares both between exporting and importing countries and among exporters. Second, the management of sector arrangements has usually been captured by producers; thus, established firms at home and abroad benefit from the arrangement, whereas new exporting firms and new exporting countries often experience curtailed growth.

In the long run, the real question concerning sector agreements is whether they promote more "organized" or more "free" trade. Few would deny a beleaguered sector temporary protection to adjust, to revive if it can, or to scale back if it must. Many would say that, if Japan organizes and protects its semiconductor market, the United States must mount an appropriate response. But how long should "temporary" trade protection and management last? Is the point of a sector arrangement to give the domestic industry a chance to compete or to ensure that the domestic industry retains a certain market share? The evidence strongly points to restrictive tendencies: Sector arrangements tend to persist for long periods, to encompass a more extensive range of products, to impose higher restrictions, to freeze market shares, and to reinforce bilateral trade flows. Because of those tendencies, sector agreements may be characterized as the dark prince of trade policy.[1]

Whether the Uruguay Round slumbers to a conclusion or makes great strides, arrangements will continue to be struck along sectoral lines between major trading countries. In 1989 the carbon steel "voluntary" restraint agreement was extended for a further thirty months; in 1991 the Multifiber Agreement is scheduled for renewal. Beyond those arrangements, deals could be made in automobiles (especially as the European Community consolidates its quotas for member countries in preparation for 1992), civilian aircraft (in an attempt to settle the dispute between Boeing and Airbus), and other sectors.

In order to understand the dynamics of sector arrangements, is it worth examining two: the Multifiber Agreement, which was designed to manage trade in the slow-growing textile and apparel industries, and the semiconductor agreement, which was designed to manage trade in a dynamic high-technology sector.

Managing Slow Growth: Textiles and Apparel

Perhaps the most remarkable feature of textile and apparel trade is the way in which producers in those basically competitive industries have for so long used their national governments to create cartels in international trade.[2]

The roots of the present arrangement can be traced to the 1930s. From 1935 to 1940, the United States limited textile imports from Japan through "voluntary" restraints, selective tariff increases, and industry-to-industry agreements. Similar restraints were imposed by the United Kingdom, France, and other industrial countries. The defeat of Japan in World War II buried the textile issue until the 1950s.

In the 1950s, however, the United Kingdom and Western Europe again erected quantitative restrictions against Japanese exports of cotton textiles. In 1956, prodded by Congress, President Dwight D. Eisenhower negotiated a five-year "voluntary" restraint agreement on Japanese cotton textile exports. In 1959, through industry-to-industry consultations, the United Kingdom extended its import restraints to suppliers of cotton fabric from Hong Kong, India, and Pakistan. These bilateral arrangements paved the way for the Short-Term Arrangement.

1. *The Short-Term Arrangement.* At the insistence of President John F. Kennedy, a series of meetings were held to discuss sector agreements. From those discussions emerged the Short-Term Arrangement (STA) Regarding International Trade in Cotton Textiles in July 1961. The STA, signed by the delegates of sixteen countries, covered sixty-four categories of cotton textiles. Its key feature was the "market-disruption" provision that was borrowed from a November 1960 GATT paper. The concept of market disruption involves a less restrictive definition of the impact on trade than the "serious injury" test required for escape-clause relief under GATT Article 19 or under U.S. law. Under the new test, projected increases in imports and differentials in the prices of domestic and imported goods were used as criteria for limiting imports.

The existence or even threat of market disruption enabled the importing country to restrain trade, unilaterally or by agreement, to a level not lower than imports during the preceding twelve-month period. In other words, the principle of "selective" country-specific export restraints was an outgrowth of the market-disruption concept. By their nature, selective restraints derogate from the most-favored-nation principle proclaimed in GATT Article 1.

2. *The Long-Term Arrangement.* The STA included machinery to create the Long-Term Arrangement (LTA)

Regarding International Trade in Cotton Textiles, which was signed by the representative of nineteen countries. The LTA, which became effective in October 1962, was a congressional precondition, contained in the Trade Expansion Act of 1962, for granting the president negotiating authority for what became the Kennedy Round of trade negotiations.[3]

The LTA covered textiles containing more than 50 percent cotton by weight or by value. The coverage of products was thereby expanded from cotton textiles to blends, and the LTA, like the STA, provided for the imposition of quotas by bilateral agreement or by the unilateral action of the importing country, but the quota could not be set at levels less than the actual goods imported during the preceding year. Under normal circumstances, quotas were supposed to allow for growth in the volume of imports by 5 percent per year.

3. *The Multifiber Agreements.* As a precondition of the Trade Act of 1974 (which gave the president negotiating authority to launch the Tokyo Round), Congress insisted on concluding the first Multifiber Agreement (MFA I) and obtaining the partial exemption of textiles from tariff cuts. MFA I entailed a further extension in the coverage of products: It extended to imports of man-made fibers and wool products, in addition to cotton textiles. MFA I appropriated from the LTA the "market-disruption" concept, the authorization to negotiate bilateral agreements, and the power to impose unilateral quotas.

As a concession to exporters, MFA I provided that any agreement pertaining to bilateral restraints must include provisions for an annual growth in the volume of imports of not less than 6 percent. It also allowed for two kinds of "flexibility provisions": the limited transferability of quotas among product categories during a particular year, known as "swing"; and the limited adjustment of the quota for a particular product from one year to another, known as "carry forward" (borrowing up to 10 percent from next year's quota) and "carry over" (carrying over up to 10 percent of a quota to a future year). In later versions of the Multifiber Agreement, all of those concessions were eroded.

In December 1977 the Protocol of 1977 extended MFA I for four years. (The protocol and MFA I together are known as MFA II.) The protocol included a provision that allowed for "reasonable departures" from the framework of MFA I with the "mutual agreement" of the importing and exporting members. In other words, an importing country was permitted to restrain the growth of imports below the customary 6 percent.

In February 1979, under pressure from the U.S. textile industry, which made its support of the Trade Agreements Act of 1979 contingent on further trade relief, the Carter administration issued a white paper that ushered in a wave of restrictions. Most important, the administration endorsed the concept set forth in the white paper that any growth in imports should be related to domestic market growth and introduced the concept that "import surges" could trigger tighter controls.

Similarly, the European Community negotiated new and stricter bilateral agreements with all its major suppliers. Other industrial countries were quick to follow suit. For the first time, industrial importers placed global ceilings on certain categories of "sensitive" products.

In December 1981, at the urging of the European Community and with the acquiescence of President Reagan, the Protocol of 1981 was negotiated. (This protocol together with MFA I is known as MFA III.) MFA III incorporated several restrictive approaches built into the Carter white paper on textile trade:

- The normal minimum import growth rate of 6 percent (in volume terms) can be abandoned for "dominant suppliers" (for example, Hong Kong, Taiwan, Korea,

Macao) when importing countries face a threat to their "minimum viable production."
• "Antisurge" clauses can be used to preclude the full utilization of previously unused quotas, with compensation to be paid on other products.
• "Market disruption" was redefined to include the overall growth of the market for the product in the importing country and thus can take into account any decline in growth resulting from shifting patterns of demand.

In July 1986 MFA IV was signed. It underscored the determination of the signatories to continue the practice of widening the scope of product coverage and plugging "leaks" in earlier versions of the MFA. MFA IV will expire in 1991.

Table 4.1 summarizes textile and apparel trade in terms of import penetration ratios that prevailed between 1975 and 1986. During a comparable period, the value of world textile and apparel exports grew from about $36 billion (1973) to $128 billion (1986). In terms of import penetration, the U.S. ratios nearly tripled; the European Community and Japanese ratios approximately doubled; while the Canadian ratios remained virtually unchanged. In other words, imports were allowed to capture a larger share of the markets of industrial countries, but the degree of policy resistance differed greatly between the United States and other industrial countries.

Because of the rapid increase in imports as a share of domestic markets, Congress became increasingly concerned. In March 1985 Congressman Ed Jenkins (D–Ga.) and Senator Strom Thurmond (R–S.C.) introduced the Textile and Apparel Trade Enforcement Act of 1985. The bill would have sharply rolled back imports from major suppliers, including Hong Kong, South Korea, and China; and it would have restricted future growth in total imports to 1 percent per year, including imports from Western Europe and other industrial countries that exported to the United States free of quotas. The Commerce Department estimated that the bill would raise prices by an average of 10 percent and would cost consumers $14 billion annually, almost $140,000 per job "saved" in the industry.[4] The bill was vetoed by President Reagan.

In 1988 a revamped version of the 1985 bill passed the House and the Senate. The fact that the textile industry was operating at 95 percent of capacity and enjoyed robust profits had little impact on Congress. Under the 1988 bill, the limit on the growth of global imports was established at 1 percent a year, compared to the 16 to 17 percent annual growth in textile imports in the mid-1980s.[5] The cost to consumers was estimated to be between $20 billion and $40 billion annually.[6] Like the 1985 bill, the 1988 legislation was vetoed by President Reagan.

Will the textile saga ever turn the page to a liberal chapter? The powerful forces maintaining the status quo should not be underestimated. Producers in developed countries fear uncertainty and competition, and producers in developing countries derive quota rents from protection. Many developing countries prefer the predictability of quotas to the opportunities of open markets. A great many bureaucrats are employed to operate the system. Despite three decades of increasing restraints, the industry is clamoring for new barriers just as loudly today as it did in the 1960s.[7]

Only with the greatest political effort, the most generous adjustment programs, and a worldwide commitment to liberalization will the MFA countries work their way out of the textile morass.[8] In the meantime, the history of the Multifiber Agreement stands as its own warning against comparable arrangements in other sectors.

Managing High-Tech: Semiconductors

The story of semiconductors is a story of how U.S. producers in a young and dynamic industry of their own creation turned to trade remedies in response to the challenge from Japan.[9] Unfortunately, as the U.S. producers discovered, trade remedies do not guarantee competitive health. In fact, they may even contribute to a decline in an industry that was supposed to benefit from them.

1. *The Battle Takes Shape.* The story begins with the U.S. invention of the integrated circuit in 1959. For the next fifteen years, U.S. companies dominated the semiconductor field. They introduced the dynamic random access memory chip (DRAM).[10] They were the first to present the new generations of DRAMs (the 4K DRAM in 1973 and the 16K DRAM in 1975), and they created the microprocessor.[11] The funding of the NASA moonshot and the Minuteman missile programs in the 1960s accelerated the development of the industry.

Early in 1957 Japan enacted the Extraordinary Measures Law for the Promotion of the Electronics Industry. That law authorized the Ministry of International Trade and Industry (MITI) to coordinate the industry to avoid duplicative research, to provide subsidies, and to create cartels if necessary. The first target of Japanese policy was the U.S. computer market. By the early 1970s, however, MITI began to accept the view that semiconductors are the linchpin of the computer industry. The computer war with the United States turned into a semiconductor war, and the main battleground became memory chips.

The Japanese companies that are fighting the battle are huge multiproduct conglomerates. Their basic strategy is based on achieving four objectives:

- To invest heavily, even when the markets are depressed, thereby creating the capacity to gain a greater market share in the next market upswing.
- To run plants at maximum capacity even if excess production results in sales that yield a loss (in the ear-

ly 1980s, Japanese firms lost about $4 billion produc-
ing memory chips).

• To cross-license their technology to other Japanese
firms (ironically, U.S. producers also licensed Japanese
companies because they considered them less dangerous
than their U.S. competitors).

• To buy chips from other Japanese firms (especially
from affiliated companies) rather than buy from U.S. or
other foreign companies.

By the end of the 1970s, through the combined use of
government guidance, brilliant engineering, and aggressive expansion, Japan was producing DRAMs at the
lowest cost in the world.[12] Since late 1981, the U.S. industry
has appealed to the government to take action. At the industry's urging, bilateral trade talks were pursued to
achieve two major objectives: (1) to prevent the dumping
of Japanese chips on the U.S. market and (2) to increase
the U.S. share of the Japanese market. Two agreements
were negotiated between Japan and the United States in
pursuit of these goals.

2. *The Semiconductor Agreements.* In mid-1982, the
Semiconductor Industry Association threatened Japan
with a Section 301 complaint, but little came of this initiative. However, a U.S.-Japan high-tech working group met
several times throughout 1983, and the result, in the First
Semiconductor Agreement, was the elimination of
Japanese tariffs (then 4 percent) on semiconductor imports.
At the same time, MITI made a loose commitment to open
the Japanese market to foreign chips.

For a few months the U.S. share of the Japanese market
increased. Then, when the worldwide collapse in the demand for chips occurred in mid-1984, many U.S. companies
(including major producers such as Intel and AT&T) left
the memory chip market.[13] But the Japanese firms,

following their strategy, continued to make chips at the same pace, investing in new facilities and cutting back on the purchase of U.S. chips. A drop in the Japanese demand of 11 percent therefore translated into a drop in U.S. sales to Japan of 30 percent. By 1985, Japanese firms had captured 70 percent of the world DRAM market (see Table 4.2).[14] In contrast, U.S. firms had begun to concentrate on more sophisticated products such as specialized logic chips, microprocessors, and erasable programmable read-only memory chips (EPROMs).[15] Accordingly, the U.S. loss of market share was not nearly so dramatic for the overall semiconductor market as it was for the memory chip market. Still, there was a decided loss. By 1986, shipments by U.S.-based companies accounted for 44 percent of the world semiconductor market, down from 54 percent in 1978, whereas shipments by Japanese-based companies accounted for 45 percent of the market, up from 28 percent in 1978 (see Table 4.3).

On the eve of the Second Semiconductor Agreement, the U.S. government was pursuing a dumping case on 256K DRAMs; U.S. companies had filed a blanket unfair trade petition under Section 301 and two dumping suits on EPROMs and 64K DRAMs; the Commerce Department and the International Trade Commission had made preliminary findings of massive dumping; the House of Representatives was urging the president to retaliate against Japan; and the cabinet was considering making decisions adverse to Japan. Buttressed by this political artillery, U.S. trade negotiators were in a position to achieve substantial results.

The Second Agreement, reached in July 1986, provided for more access to the Japanese market and an end to dumping.[16] The agreement reflected the contention that U.S. producers were unfairly restricted in their sales to Japan: While U.S. producers had consistently held a share of the world semiconductor market outside Japan of about

50 percent, their share of the Japanese market remained static at 10 percent. Under the terms of the agreement, MITI would encourage long-term relationships between Japanese computer firms and U.S. chip suppliers. In a confidential letter of understanding, the Japanese government acknowledged the U.S. semiconductor industry's estimation that foreign countries could achieve a 20 percent share of the market by 1991.

Apart from market-access issues, the other goal of the Second Agreement was to prevent the dumping of semiconductors by Japanese manufacturers at prices below cost not only in the United States but also in other countries. The question of how to determine whether prices are below cost is highly disputatious in a dynamic industry such as semiconductors, where outlays for research and development are enormous and where the length of production runs is uncertain. Difficult questions concerning the allocation of costs were, however, swept aside; the U.S. industry wanted higher prices, and Japan eventually acquiesced.

The initial results of the agreement were minimal, and in April 1987 the Reagan administration imposed retaliatory measures: 100 percent tariffs on $300 million of imported Japanese electronic products. MITI then implemented effective production and export controls and pushed Japanese conglomerates to integrate foreign semiconductors in their products. In order to ensure higher prices, the Japanese government created a Japanese producers' cartel. Between the fourth quarter of 1986 and the second quarter of 1988, the average price of a 256K DRAM rose from $2.10 to $3.80.[17] At the end of 1987, the trade covered by U.S. retaliatory measures was reduced to $165 million of imports; but despite pleas from Japan, these sanctions remained unchanged throughout 1988 because only limited progress had been achieved in obtaining greater access to the Japanese market.[18] In fact, in March

1989, when the Bush administration complained that Japan was not living up to its commitment, Japan denied any "legally binding agreement" with respect to market share. In 1988 American-based firms held a 10.7 percent share of the Japanese market. Under a linear progression for reaching the supposedly agreed (but now disputed) 1991 level of 20 percent, U.S. companies should have captured 14 percent of the market in 1988.

Practically no one is happy with the pact. The Semiconductor Industry Association and the American Electronics Association continue to call for more access to the Japanese market.[19] U.S. computer makers have asked for the elimination of the current floor price system used to enforce the pact's antidumping provisions.[20] The European Community has complained that Japan substantially raised prices for those chips that are not made in Western Europe while continuing to dump those chips that are made by Western European suppliers.[21]

3. *A Different Strategy: Sematech and U.S. Memories.* Quite apart from the attempt to deal with the grievances of the U.S. computer industry and Western European firms, the enforcement of the agreement has hardly improved the position of U.S. semiconductor firms in world competition. The immediate problem stems from the fact that any induced increase in chip prices probably benefits Japanese producers more than their U.S. counterparts. Japanese firms produce larger volumes of chips than U.S. producers, and so a rise in chip prices yields a greater amount of new profit to them; they are prepared to allocate a significant fraction of their profits to outlays for research and development for the next generation of chips; meanwhile, they are using excess chip capacity for their own downstream electronics products.

The deeper problem relates to the fact that trade restraints are very blunt instruments for addressing the

fundamental difficulty: the fact that the U.S. industry contains many small- and medium-sized firms that cannot afford the exceedingly high outlays for research and development that are required for each new generation of chips.
Only three U.S. companies are large vertically integrated
conglomerates (IBM, AT&T, and Texas Instruments),
whereas the entire Japanese industry consists of such
firms. By early 1988, owing to this basic difference, the
Japanese industry had captured the lead in twelve of
twenty-five key semiconductor technologies and had
achieved the same level of technological proficiency as the
U.S. industry in eight others.[22]

To remain in the race the United States must either
learn to sidestep its own antitrust laws (especially the
private treble-damage antitrust suit) and accept a more
concentrated industry, or it must develop an effective
system for inducing cooperative research on the part of
small- and medium-sized U.S. firms. In fact, under the umbrella of Sematech and U.S. Memories, the United States
is doing a little of both.[23]

Sematech (Semiconductor Manufacturing Technology)
is a research-and-development consortium whose annual
budget of $250 million is jointly funded by industry
members (50 percent) and the U.S. government (50 percent). Sematech also serves as an umbrella organization
for horizontal cooperation among chip producers and vertical cooperation between chip producers and chip buyers.[24]
U.S. Memories is a consortium of computer manufacturing firms that plan to produce 4-megabit DRAMs. Among
the thirty sponsors are Advanced Micro Devices, Digital
Equipment, Hewlett Packard, IBM, and National Semiconductor. The plan calls for $500–$600 million of equity
capital, with no sponsor furnishing more than 10 percent
of the total.

Sematech and U.S. Memories could be harbingers of
more interventionist U.S. industrial policies.[25] Proponents

of the new approach argue that, at the end of the twentieth century, comparative advantage in high-tech sectors will reflect the implementation of public policies in taxation, education, and business regulation, not endowments of natural resources or the "invisible hand" of market forces. They contend that Japanese success primarily stems from outcome-oriented policies—the reverse of process-oriented policies implemented in the United States.

To be sure, many skeptics doubt that the United States can succeed in the realm of industrial policy,[26] but if Sematech or U.S. Memories manages to revive U.S. fortunes in the semiconductor industry, a new policy model could emerge. In contrast to an indefinite succession of trade agreements, these joint ventures represent a more promising response to one of the underlying problems of international competition—the fact that many U.S. firms are too small to conduct research at the frontier of technology.

Coping with Sector Arrangements

Sector arrangements will not disappear during the 1990s. Those that protect older industries—where comparative advantage is shifting to developing countries—will be kept to slow the inevitable adjustments. Those that bolster emerging high-tech industries will be kept to provide an auxiliary off-budget stimulant.[27] Based on an acceptance of these facts of political and economic life, the Economic Summit powers should announce certain principles that will enable a more liberal trading system to emerge by the early years of the next century.

First, quantitative restraints should be converted to tariffs or auctioned quotas. For mature, low-tech industries, such as textiles and apparel, the revenues derived from such sources should be allocated to adjustment measures. For emerging high-tech industries, such as semiconductors, the revenues should be used to support joint research-and-development efforts (for example, Sematech).

Second, all countries that participate in sector agreements should make commitments to liberalize their imports. In mature sectors, this obligation should extend to Mexico and China as well as to the United States and the European Community. For high-tech sectors, this obligation should extend to Japan as well as to the United States. A reasonable target for the growth of imports should be set at 1 to 3 percent of the market annually until complete liberalization is achieved. Such targets should be accepted not only by countries that use "voluntary" restraint agreements and outright quotas to limit imports (such as the United States, Brazil, and India) but also by countries that rely on vertical integration and closed distribution systems to limit imports (such as Japan) and countries that rely on government procurement (such as the Federal Republic of Germany) to protect domestic industries, for example, telecommunications.

Third, through detailed bilateral negotiations, level playing fields should be established by the United States and Japan and the United States and the European Community for such high-tech industries as financial services, biotechnology, telecommunications, semiconductors, and civilian aircraft.[28] The level playing fields may involve detailed cross-licensing arrangements, comparable antitrust laws, equal access to government procurement, equivalent patent and copyright practices, and the careful monitoring of outcomes as well as processes. In these complex negotiations, trade policy can play an effective role in ensuring the achievement of level playing fields, but trade restrictions and market-sharing arrangement should not become ends in themselves.

Chapter 5

Retaliation: The Avenging Angel

Retaliation has an old if not quite honorable tradition in the history of trade policy. In the late nineteenth century, retaliatory tariffs spread from Italy to Austria to Germany to France. In the 1920s, and in the 1930s with a vengeance, one country after another hiked its tariffs. After the U.S. enactment of the Smoot-Hawley Tariff in 1930, retaliatory action became widespread: Spain imposed prohibitive tariffs on imports of automobiles and other products; Switzerland sponsored a boycott of U.S. products; and Canada limited the import of 125 major products.[1]

Retaliation during the 1930s gave trade warfare a bad name. A major purpose of GATT was to forestall retaliatory epidemics that would destroy trade. In the first postwar decades, episodes of retaliation were rare. The best-known instance was the "Chicken War" of 1963–64. It began when the United States greatly increased its exports of poultry to Western Europe. In order to reinforce its Common Agricultural Policy, the European Economic Community applied a higher tariff than the rate bound in GATT; and the United States brought a complaint to GATT. After a panel finding, the United States retaliated by imposing higher duties on imports of brandy, trucks, starch, and dextrine. The fallout harmed innocent parties, such as Spain, but neither side gave way. The Chicken War seemed to confirm the lesson of the 1930s: Retaliation destroys trade.[2]

Nevertheless, beginning in the 1970s, the United States began a major retaliatory campaign against "unfair imports." The instruments of reprisal were countervailing duties against subsidized goods, antidumping duties against goods sold below cost, and exclusion orders against pirated or counterfeit goods. All these remedies dated from earlier eras: The first law on countervailing duty was enacted in 1897; the antidumping law originated in 1916; and Section 337 (protection accorded to intellectual property) was enacted in 1930. But only with the provisions of the Trade Act of 1974 were those remedies made readily available to private companies without the need to obtain the U.S. government's acquiescence in prosecuting a case.

The Trade Act of 1974 inspired a multitude of cases involving unfair trade practices. Between 1974 and early 1986, the count of cases initiated was as follows: cases involving countervailing duties, 313; cases involving antidumping duties, 389; cases involving Section 337, 239—a total of 941 cases, or more than an average of 80 a year.[3]

Not only was there a vast escalation in the number of cases, but there was also a qualitative shift in the perception of such actions. Before 1970 subsidies and dumping were regarded as economic offenses. In textbook fashion these practices were viewed as inflicting economic distortion that harmed the exporting nation as much if not more than the importing nation. For example, subsidies wasted the exporting nation's own resources; while dumping—in the classical sense of selling abroad cheaper than at home—penalized domestic consumers. Everyone lost as a result of economic distortion, and it was considered the common task of civilized nations to limit such practices.

By the late 1970s and early 1980s, however, cases involving subsidies and dumping had acquired moral overtones. The practices were no longer viewed as economic offenses; they were perceived as "unfair" trade, almost the equiv-

RETALIATION   127

alent of economic warfare waged against the importing nation. Once the American public accepted the belief that "unfair" foreign trade policies were responsible for huge U.S. merchandise trade deficits, reasoned debate over the economic aspects of subsidies and dumping became far more difficult. What public official wants to defend "unfair" imports? Equally important, this shift in perception enabled a disjunction between the offense and the remedy. No longer were remedies confined to the countervailing duties or antidumping duties that had been designed precisely to offset the distortion; the new remedies included market-sharing cartels such as those established to govern the world semiconductor and carbon steel markets.

At the same time, the range of practices labeled unfair by the countervailing duty and antidumping duty statutes was vastly expanded at the behest of certain U.S. industries. Economic policy measures of ancient vintage became suspect if they affected traded goods. For example, regional grants provided to attract a new industry or adjustment subsidies expanded to wind down an old industry became prima facie "unfair." The widespread practice of selling below the fully allocated costs of production (including a "proper" allocation for sunk costs—capital costs and research-and-development expenses) could lead to a charge of dumping, despite the fact that sunk costs must be ignored when markets are soft or the product is no longer popular.

By the early 1980s, therefore, the United States had established a substantial record of targeted retaliation, which was replete with moral overtones, motivated by private petitions, and directed against unfair *imports*. Two things happened in the mid-1980s: the addition of the "remedy" of retaliation against unfair *export* barriers to the list of privately available remedies and a much more active *government* sponsorship of targeted measures designed to open foreign markets.[4]

The statutory vehicle for attacking foreign export barriers is Section 301, an omnibus measure that gives the president broad retaliatory authority. Investigations of unfair trade practices can be initiated in response to a petition filed either by an interested party or by the U.S. trade representative (USTR). If the action violates the international legal rights of the United States, the foreign practice is called "unjustifiable"; in other cases, it is considered either "unreasonable" or "discriminatory."

Between the enactment of the Trade Act of 1974 and late 1985, approximately twenty-seven export cases were brought under Section 301. Only since 1986, however, has the statute been used aggressively to retaliate against foreign barriers to U.S. exports. Between 1986 and 1988, eleven cases involving a large volume of trade were been initiated, most with government support. The cases included pharmaceutical practices in Brazil and mobile telephones in Japan. By December 1988, more than $4 billion of trade was subject to potential sanctions under Section 301.[5]

The Omnibus Trade and Competitiveness Act of 1988 served to reinforce the Reagan administration's tough new policy under Section 301. The 1988 act set forth procedural rules and deadlines for action by the USTR under Section 301 and created a new "Super 301" to address systemic unfair trade practices by foreign countries.

In May 1989, U.S. Trade Representative Carla Hills, speaking for the Bush administration, fired this new weapon with a clap heard around the world.[6] Japan, India, and Brazil were singled out as targets for market access negotiations. Six trade barriers were targeted for removal: (1) restrictive Japanese government procurement of satellites; (2) restrictive Japanese government procurement of supercomputers; (3) restrictive Japanese standards on forest products used in construction; (4) Indian restrictions of foreign insurance; (5) Indian restrictions on foreign investment; and (6) Brazil's import licensing system.

Under the Super 301 legislation, the USTR has twelve to eighteen months to negotiate away these barriers before imposing retaliatory measures.

Another eight countries were put on a "priority watch list" for their inadequate protection of intellectual property. The priority countries are Brazil, India, South Korea, Mexico, China, Saudi Arabia, Taiwan, and Thailand. Progress in negotiations with these countries will be reviewed in 150 days. (By November 1989, South Korea, Taiwan, and Saudi Arabia were judged by the USTR to be making satisfactory progress.) Another seventeen countries were also cited for their intellectual property practices, and negotiations with those nations are to be reviewed after eleven months.

These actions prompted widespread foreign criticism of the United States. But negotiations soon started with many countries, and even before the Super 301 actions were announced, South Korea and Taiwan lifted some trade barriers in order to keep their names off the list of "hard-core" offenders.

Central to the use of retaliation as a tool of trade policy are two questions. Will a country benefit from threatening (or actually imposing) retaliatory measures to induce its trading partner to alter "unfair" practices? Or will the initiator lose, both economically and politically, by prompting countermeasures and by creating acrimony?[7]

Examples of both positive and negative outcomes can be cited. The constructive use of retaliatory threats is illustrated by the U.S. response to the enlarged European Community. When Portugal and Spain joined the European Community in March 1986, the European Community did three things that offended U.S. sensibilities: First, the European Community imposed restrictions on the importation into Portugal of oilseeds and oilseed products; second, it required that a specific portion of Portuguese imports of grain be reserved for suppliers from other members of the European Community; third, it withdrew tariff concessions and imposed variable levies on sorghum imports.

The value of U.S. exports affected by those European Community actions exceeded $1 billion annually.[8] On March 31, 1986, President Reagan announced retaliatory measures that would affect a comparable level of exports from the European Community to the United States unless the dispute could be resolved through negotiations. The affected U.S. imports were so-called yuppie goods such as Perrier water and fine cheeses. Eventually, in January 1987, the European Community and the United States reached a four-year interim agreement. The European Community committed itself to import two million tons of corn and 300,000 tons of sorghum annually at reduced levies and to lower customs duties on a range of industrial and processed agricultural goods. The European Community also renounced its minimum reserved share of the Portuguese cereals market, representing about 450,000 tons. In return, the United States canceled its yuppie tariffs. In this case, the threat of U.S. retaliation was sufficient to cause the European Community to lower prospective trade barriers.

But there have been instances when retaliatory threats did not work. For example, on October 21, 1988, following well-ventilated acrimony, President Reagan levied 100 percent tariffs against certain Brazilian products in retaliation for the infringement of U.S. pharmaceutical patents by Brazilian firms. Brazil defiantly accepted the U.S. sanctions rather than abandon its long-standing policy of not granting patent protection for pharmaceuticals.[9] Since then, Brazil has initiated a GATT case to vindicate its rights.

Although the United States has emphasized unilateral retaliation, it has also tried to devise multilateral solutions under GATT auspices. For example, since the late

1970s the United States persistently tried to pressure Tokyo into opening its domestic market to farm imports, especially beef and citrus. Finally, as a face-saving device, the parties agreed to take their dispute to GATT. After a GATT panel found that twelve Japanese agricultural restrictions were illegal, Japan agreed to scrap ten of them and to pay compensation for the other two. Some of the quota restraints will be converted into tariffs. Thus, following years of bilateral pressure, the Japanese beef and citrus markets will finally be open, in a limited way, to foreign goods.

Other countries have also tried GATT procedures to address unfair trade practices. In recent months, for example, Australia won a GATT panel determination against U.S. sugar quotas and has threatened to bring another GATT panel against the U.S. Meat Import Act of 1964.[10] Japan has initiated a GATT hearing over the application of European Community dumping procedures against "screwdriver plants."[11] The European Community has initiated a GATT inquiry against Hyundai Merchant Marine of Korea involving the novel issue of predatory policies in the services sector.[12]

In a current case of retaliation and counterretaliation, the European Community proposed, as a health measure, to close its common market on December 31, 1988, to beef containing certain hormones.[13] This restriction would cost U.S. exporters $100 million in lost sales. In response, the United States imposed duties of up to 100 percent on a wide range of European Community foodstuff exports worth about $100 million (boneless beef and pork, fruit juice, wine coolers, canned tomatoes, cheese, and instant coffee), effective January 1, 1989. The European Community Council of Ministers then voted to counterretaliate by February 20, 1989, and to impose 100 percent duties against $100 million worth of U.S. exports of shelled walnuts and dried fruits. But the council also voted to delay implementation of the new measures to allow negotiators time to find a compromise solution. A binational task force was then set up to examine ways in which the United States could resume shipments of European Community-certified hormone-free beef (the European Community had earlier agreed to allow imports of beef certified to be hormone-free by the state authorities of Texas) and to find a lasting solution to the dispute. Hormones are now out of the headlines—thanks in part to the draconian import restrictions imposed in early 1989 by the United States against Chilean fruit, in the wake of a cyanide scare. Careful management of retaliation and counterretaliation in the hormone case, coupled with the Chilean fruit episode, seems to have yielded grudging U.S. acceptance that trade restrictions can be based on health concerns, however "irrational."

Retaliation, undertaken unilaterally and multilaterally, has become a staple part of the world trading system. Retaliation can serve to pry open inaccessible markets, to curtail the infringement of intellectual property, to curb dumping and subsidies, and to resolve difficult health and safety disputes. But retaliation can get out of control in economic terms, and it can poison relations in political terms. What can be done to manage the retaliatory elements of the trading system? Three suggestions are offered.

First, with an improvement in the GATT dispute system at hand, and with the extension of GATT rules to new areas, more episodes should be channeled multilaterally. The major advantage of GATT procedures stems from the fact that the losing country can more gracefully accept the findings of an international panel and thus become more willing to change its practices.

Second, the GATT Secretariat should monitor all the retaliatory actions of member countries and publish an annual enumeration and evaluation of ongoing cases.

Estimates should be made of the trade coverage involved in disputes, any trade liberalization achieved, and the magnitude of retaliation. Such a review would give both officials and journalists a better appreciation of the constructive and the destructive uses of retaliation.

Third, the Group of Seven Summit countries should quietly agree to consign retaliation to the status of a side show in the trading system. It is fair to observe that the United States today is more dissatisfied with the trading system than it was in 1974—despite the enormous increase in cases involving countervailing duties, antidumping, and Section 301. Seldom does retaliation give complete satisfaction; one helping of retaliation can easily inspire the appetite for a second; and the process of retaliation can distract from cooperative efforts at trade liberalization. The Group of Seven Summit leaders have everything to gain by keeping retaliation off center stage.

Chapter 6

Free Trade Areas:
White Knights

If sector agreements are the "dark prince" of trade policy and retaliation is the "avenging angel," then free trade areas are the "white knights." Whereas producers gain the upper hand in most sector agreements, in free trade areas and customs unions, consumer interests usually prevail.[1] In retaliatory episodes, even when barriers are brought down, bad feelings linger. By contrast, free trade areas can promote warm relations among participants.

Equally important, free trade areas often succeed in demolishing deep-seated structural barriers. Within the European Community, for example, government procurement practices, rights of establishment, and common standards for high-tech products are now being addressed. Australia and New Zealand have launched a program to harmonize competition policy, consumer protection statutes, and copyright laws. Finally, there is the "magnetism" of a thriving free trade area. As time passes, existing members may welcome policy harmonization in new areas, and their success might well prompt other countries to join. In 1989, for example, militarily neutral Austria announced it would apply for membership in the European Community. "Euromagnetism" is already strong enough to overcome even such a severe political obstacle as neutrality. "Magnetism" is the property that propels existing free trade areas to serve as foundation stones for an even larger OECD free trade and investment area.

Ever since Jacob Viner's classic work was published,[2] economists have agonized over the question whether a free trade area diverts more trade from third countries than it creates among its own members.[3] In fact, even the remote possibility of trade diversion is part of the magnetic allure of a vital free trade area: The prospect of trade diversion prompts other countries to seek to affiliation with the group, and the end result is to enlarge the zone of liberalization.

It is worth reviewing three free trade areas in order to understand the forces of liberalization and magnetism that are at work: the European Community of 1992; the U.S.-Canada Free Trade Agreement; and the Australia–New Zealand Closer Economic Relations Agreement.

Completion of the European Community Internal Market in 1992

In 1957 six countries in Western Europe signed the Treaty of Rome, which established a customs union based on the vision of an integrated continental market. In the 1970s and 1980s, the Europe of the Six was enlarged to the Europe of the Nine, then of the Ten, and now a Europe of the Twelve.[4] In 1985, the leaders of the European Community set the ambitious goal of translating the 1957 vision of a continental market into reality by 1992. Like the continental U.S. market, the internal market of the European Community will be free of obstacles to the movement of goods, persons, services, and capital. Successful integration will create one of the largest unified markets in the world based on a population of 320 million and a GDP of $4,300 billion (1988 figures).

During the 1960s tariffs were dismantled within the European Community. But at the same time, the member nations not only retained a multitude of nontariff barriers but also erected others. The program set forth in the 1985 white paper for 1992 contemplates the enactment of approximately three hundred directives to create a barrier-free internal market.[5]

To facilitate the implementation of the white paper and to counter the paralyzing slowness of the European Community's decision making machinery, the Single European Act was passed at the end of 1985 and became effective in mid-1987. The act permits almost all directives to be adopted by qualified majority voting rather than a unanimous vote cast by the member states. (The significant exceptions involve taxation, the free movement of persons, and employee rights.) The act also grants the European Commission wider executive power to implement rules authorized by the Council of Ministers. (The commission is essentially the European Community's executive body: It drafts proposals for council decision and ensures the application of the Treaty of Rome and subsidiary legislation in the member states.)

Another factor contributing to momentum was a council accord on a medium-term solution to the European Community's budgetary impasse and a doubling of "structural funds" for depressed regions. The accord enabled officials to turn their attention from immediate budget problems; it also alleviated fears that the completion of the internal market would worsen regional disparities.[6]

As of May 1989, the internal market program envisaged the adoption of 279 directives. Some 117 of these have already been adopted in their entirety by the Council of Ministers, an additional 5 have been partially adopted, and a further 11 have been broadly accepted by the council. Another 99 proposals have been drafted by the commission and await the attention of the council. Finally 47 proposals are still under consideration within the commission. This speed is remarkable. Progress on minor matters was easy to achieve; but in addition to items such as common rules for price labels in shops and levels of pesticide residue in foodstuffs, the council has adopted directives dealing with more difficult topics such as air transport, vehicle emissions, insurance, and the liberalization of capital movements.[7] European success demonstrates how much easier it is to convince twelve trading partners of the benefits to be derived from eliminating deep structural protection than to persuade ninety-seven GATT members.

Detailed estimates of the costs and benefits of an integrated Western European market were made in a study directed by Paolo Cecchini.[8] The report estimates that over the medium term, the single market could boost the European Community's GDP by between 4.5 percent and 7 percent and could increase employment by 1.8 million to 5 million persons.

In business terms who will gain from the growth? The European Commission has declared that European Community firms, not outsiders, should be the main beneficiaries. In areas where international obligations do not now exist, one spokesman, Willy de Clercq, stated that "the EC sees no reason why the benefits of their internal liberalizations should be extended unilaterally to third countries."[9]

Outside Europe and especially in the United States this attitude arouses concern.[10] Concern is based on the apprehension that the European bureaucracy, as it formulates commercial and industrial directives in those areas that are untouched by international rules, will devise solutions that meet the demands of its protectionist members. The result could be new and greater discrimination that will negate not only U.S. export opportunities but also diminish the prospects of U.S. firms doing business within the European Community.

Much will depend on the detailed compromises that will be made to achieve a free internal market and whether the protectionist voices of France, Italy, and Spain will overcome the free trade voices of the Federal Republic of Germany, the Netherlands, and the United Kingdom in making these compromises.

In September 1988, Prime Minister Margaret Thatcher left no doubt about her determination to block any "progress" in the integration of the European Community that would involve more regulation.[11] With less drama but equal determination, the West German government declared its strong opposition to new trade restraints as a price of integration.[12] Such pronouncements may take the edge off U.S. concerns, but they do not allay all the fears. The deepest concerns of U.S. firms involve trade in areas where current GATT rules are weak or nonexistent, notably banking and telecommunications. There is, however, a silver lining to looming conflicts: Their resolution could well entail agreements that eventually eliminate behind-the-border protection on both sides of the Atlantic.

1. *Banking.* As part of the integrated economy that is planned for 1992, the European Community is seeking the wholesale liberalization of financial services.[13] Two principles are involved. First, a firm chartered in one member country, and supervised by that country's authorities, would have the right to do business in all member countries. Second, with respect to non-European Community suppliers of financial services, the European Community asserts that the principle of reciprocity should apply: Foreign banks that conduct business in the European Community should enjoy the same access that European Community banks are permitted in the foreign country. Both principles (reciprocity and home country responsibility for supervision) are part of the Second Banking Directive, currently under consideration.

The principle of reciprocity echoes the call for "level playing fields" so often heard in the United States. In the case of banking, however, the United States is reluctant to subscribe to the principle of reciprocity. The traditional separation between banking and commerce embodied in the Glass-Steagall Act of 1933 prohibits U.S. banks from providing the full range of financial services that European Community banks offer (for example, insurance and securities brokerage), and the McFadden Act of 1927 severely limits banking across state lines. Faced with this dilemma, the United States has advocated the principle of national treatment: Foreign banks operating within the European Community should be permitted the same range of powers as European banks; whereas European Community banks operating in the United States should have the same (more limited) range of powers as U.S. banks. The fact that U.S. banks are more limited in their powers than Western European banks should not, according to U.S. views, undermine the principle of national treatment.

The European Community was of two minds about the competing merits of the national treatment principle and the reciprocity principle. The finance ministers of several northern countries, including the Federal Republic of Germany, Luxembourg, the Netherlands, and the United Kingdom, were very skeptical about reciprocity. But France and Belgium supported reciprocity as a "non-protectionist" means of opening up world financial markets.

In the end, European Community officials indicated that they would seek pragmatic ways of ensuring that U.S. bank activities within the European Community are not impeded.[14] Quite possibly the trans-Atlantic dialogue could eventually contribute to the amendment of the Glass-Steagall and McFadden Acts, a substantial extension of bank powers within the United States, and far greater competition in the financial services market. Meanwhile, European insistence on substantial reciprocity could prompt Japan to liberalize its financial markets at a more rapid pace.

2. *Telecommunications.* During the 1980s, telecommunications became a major subject of trade conflict between the United States and the European Community.[15] The episode began in January 1984, with the landmark judgment that led to the divestiture of AT&T from its local operating companies. As a result, the U.S. domestic market for telecommunications equipment was suddenly opened to foreign competition. Western European governments, however, continued to protect their own home markets and vigorously promoted the exports of telecommunications equipment. The imbalance led to sharp criticism in Congress and culminated in the telecommunications provisions of the Omnibus Trade and Competitiveness Act of 1988.

The 1988 act requires the U.S. trade representative to identify "priority foreign countries" whose policies and practices deny fair market access to telecommunications equipment and services offered by U.S. companies. The USTR was instructed to complete its investigation by January 23, 1989, and to submit its report within thirty days. At the end of a three-year negotiating period, if agreement is not reached with a priority country, the president is authorized to retaliate.[16]

On February 11, U.S. Trade Representative Carla Hills named the European Community nations and South Korea as "priority countries" for telecommunications negotiations. The main targets within the European Community are France and the Federal Republic of Germany, where the barriers are the greatest. One source has speculated that a bilateral deal might be possible if the United States agreed to remove its Buy America provisions on military procurement in exchange for gaining access to European telecommunications procurement.

In any event, the European Community now subscribes to the view that the completion of the internal market requires efficient information systems and services. Consequently, in June 1987 the European Commission issued a green paper that proposed a series of measures to liberalize telecommunications equipment and services.[17] The green paper, however, left ample room for discrimination by setting forth the goals of "safeguarding the financial viability of Telecommunications Administrations" and "preserving the monopoly of PTTs [posts, telephones, and telegraphs] in the provision of network equipment." In the U.S. view, those phrases carry strong protectionist connotations.[18]

Subsequent actions suggest less European Community protectionism rather than more. In June 1988, the Council of Telecommunications Ministers took the first step to open the European Community's heavily regulated telecommunications markets by adopting common technical standards. From 1992 on, the governments of member states must grant foreign and domestic bidders the same treatment in the market for telecommunications equipment. Other harbingers of a more liberal outlook can be seen. In February 1989, for example, Italy's principal state holding company approved a plan for AT&T to become a partner with Italtel S.p.A., the state-owned telecommunications equipment manufacturer. AT&T was chosen among three European competitors (Siemens AG of West Germany, Ericsson Telefon of Sweden, and Alcatel N.V. of the Netherlands) to help overhaul Italy's antiquated telephone network. Analysts estimate that Italy will spend about $12 billion on switching and transmission equipment and that Italtel will win about half those orders. Likewise, in March 1989, the European Community council refused to approve a directive that would have required a minimum of 60 percent of the programs broadcast by European Community television and cable stations to be of European Community-origin. Instead, European Community ministers agreed on rules that seek, "where practical," to devote a majority of air time to European programs.

Quite possibly the convergence between the European Community's push for liberalization and the U.S. demand for market access will lead to an almost level playing field in the telecommunications markets of the 1990s. If that turns out to be the outcome, credit will be due to the combined thrust of the European Community and the telecommunications provisions of the 1988 Omnibus Act.

U.S.-Canada Free Trade Agreement

Historic Canadian elections, held on November 21, 1988, assured the ratification of the U.S.-Canada Free Trade Agreement by the Canadian Parliament.[19] The FTA entered into force on January 1, 1989. This agreement represents the culmination of almost 150 years of uneven economic relations between the two countries that began with Great Britain's termination of colonial preferences in 1846. Since then economic relations have been characterized by several flirtations with freer trade (notably, in 1891, 1911, and 1946) and several bouts of retaliatory trade actions.[20]

In the 1988 election, the opposition Liberal party and the New Democrat party attempted to exploit fears that the FTA would enable the United States to "take over" Canada in three areas:

- Multinational corporations operating in the energy sector would extend their reach into Canada's rich but increasingly hard-to-extract energy resources.
- The principle of national treatment in the field of investment would offer unlimited opportunity for U.S. firms to increase their stakes in Canada, a country where foreigners now own a larger share of domestic business than in any other industrialized economy.
- Generous Canadian programs in the area of social welfare would be "watered down to the lowest common denominator," namely U.S. standards. This would happen because the FTA would encourage Canadian firms

to relocate in the United States to escape higher Canadian taxes or because U.S. firms would launch countervailing duty actions against Canadian social welfare programs.

In addition to those arguments, nightmare scenarios were sketched: For example, it was said that the FTA might be used to divert water from Canada's many lakes and bays to the American Southwest, and it was argued that Canada would become a "cultural colony" of Hollywood.

Despite those arguments, Canadians took a "leap of faith" and rejected the proposition that the FTA would fatally assault their national sovereignty and cultural identity.[21] The bargain struck between Canada and the United States might provide inspiration for future bilateral agreements, for example, between the United States and Mexico.[22] Three achievements of the agreement deserve special mention because they go well beyond the probable accomplishments of the Uruguay Round: tariffs and customs, energy, and contingent protection.

1. *Tariffs and Customs.* The FTA will eliminate all tariffs between Canada and the United States within a ten-year period.[23] This is not a small accomplishment even though by 1987 approximately 80 percent of Canadian exports had already entered the U.S. market duty free, and 65 percent of U.S. exports had entered Canada duty free. The remaining tariffs covered "sensitive" sectors, such as Canadian machinery, and their prospective elimination entailed significant political sacrifices. In addition, various miscellaneous matters relating to customs were settled. For example, both parties agreed to eliminate duty drawbacks paid on imports from third countries so that trans-shipped goods would not derive advantage from the bilateral accord.

In economic terms the elimination of tariffs is probably the most important part of the FTA. Once all tariff cuts have been implemented, U.S. exports to Canada might increase by $2.4 billion, whereas Canadian exports might increase by about $1.1 billion.[24] Induced employment growth in Canada has been estimated in the range of 120,000 jobs, whereas the figure for the United States is about 30,000 jobs.[25] Calculations of real GNP gains to Canada range from 2.5 percent to 3.5 percent, whereas the gains to the United States have been estimated at a fraction of 1 percent.[26]

2. *Energy: Assured Supply and Market Access.* The energy chapter of the FTA covers more the $8 billion of trade per year consisting mostly of Canadian exports to the United States.[27] The agreement succeeded in applying the spirit of GATT to trade in energy products.

Before the 1970s, when energy resources were readily available on world markets, Canadian exporters were often denied access to the U.S. market; after the oil crisis, when energy resources were suddenly scarce, the Canadian government restricted exports to the United States. The FTA developed a framework for liberalization that applies to both imports and exports. With respect to imports, the FTA treats energy like other products subject to normal GATT discipline rather than as a "special status" good. The FTA thus rules out the use of quantitative restrictions and minimum import prices and puts some limits on internal price control measures. The FTA also tightened the exceptions to free trade that are allowed for reasons of national security.

With respect to exports, the FTA prohibits taxes on energy exports that do not bear equally on those products destined for domestic consumption. The FTA also mandates that, just as the importer is obligated to provide market access when prices are low, the exporter is obligated to provide supplies when prices are high. The exporting country may not set a higher price for exports than for domestic sales.

The FTA energy deal illustrates the kind of bargain that would be exceedingly hard to negotiate on a global basis within GATT. Canada gained assured access to markets, thereby enhancing its prospects to obtain the large investments needed to exploit its high-cost energy reserves. On the other side of the border, the United States significantly improved its long-term energy security.

3. *Contingent Protection and the Settlement of Disputes.* The phrase "contingent protection" was coined by Ambassador Rodney Grey, a Canadian trade negotiator, to describe countervailing duty, antidumping duty, and other import-limiting actions imposed on a semidiscretionary basis. A study of the record reveals why contingent protection was so important to Canada in the free trade negotiations. Between 1980 and 1986, Canada faced ten countervailing duty petitions, and about 5 percent of Canadian merchandise exports were subject to penalty duties or adverse settlements. In addition, Canada faced approximately seventeen antidumping cases between 1980 and 1986.[28] In the Canadian view, U.S. contingent protection not only interrupts trade, but also jeopardizes investment projects in Canada because access to the U.S. market can seemingly be cut off at any time.

The FTA did not phase out countervailing or antidumping duties or significantly alter the escape clause. But the FTA did begin to formulate "rules of the game" for using those measures. Disputes will be subject to a process that includes notification, the provision of information, consultation, referral to a joint commission, and finally arbitration.[29] Moreover, the parties are committed to three main undertakings: negotiating jointly accepted rules for defining subsidies and dumping practices, permitting the other party to review changes made in existing antidumping and countervailing duty laws, and establishing binational panels to supplement internal judicial review of countervailing and antidumping actions. These review and dispute settlement procedures go well beyond the past or prospective achievements of GATT.

Australia–New Zealand
Closer Economic Relations Agreement

For many decades, Australia and New Zealand were the most protectionist countries in the OECD area with respect to manufactured goods.[30] Since the early 1960s, however, Australia and New Zealand have implemented two major agreements that dramatically liberalized trans-Tasmanian trade.[31] The New Zealand–Australia Free Trade Agreement (NAFTA), which operated from 1966 to 1982, reduced tariff barriers across a limited range of products. The far more extensive Australia–New Zealand Closer Economic Relations Agreement, which became effective in January 1983, covers all goods unless specifically excepted and a wide range of services. It dismantles protective barriers according to a prearranged timetable.

In August 1988 the two prime ministers signed several protocols to expand the CER to cover sectors such as finance, transportation, and services and to provide for further liberalization such as the freedom of movement between the two countries. Both nations agreed upon the gradual and automatic removal of all frontier barriers to trade in manufactured and agricultural goods by July 1990, five years ahead of the original timetable. By 1990 there will be a single market in goods, services, and commercial dealings across the Tasmanian Sea.

To help ensure a level playing field, the two countries simultaneously committed themselves to harmonize their competition laws. Additional protocols and agreements ensure an alignment of quarantine procedures, the harmonization of business law, the elimination of technical barriers to trade, the removal of export prohibitions, and the abolition of various anticompetitive subsidy measures.

Difficult negotiations concerning investment, taxation, and trans-Tasmanian shipping remain. But the CER already underscores an economic relationship unequaled in recent years between sovereign countries.

Chapter 7

An OECD Free Trade and Investment Area

Each free trade area and common market is unique in its political setting, its purpose, and its arrangements. Yet, because of their "magnetic" character, the existing free trade areas and common markets could well provide the foundation for integrating the world economy starting with a new twenty-first century OECD Free Trade and Investment Area.[1] The OECD FTIA would have several attractive features. It would encompass countries that embrace common democratic principles and countries whose economies are very much alike in terms of standards of living, social security systems, and environmental protection. It would soften the edges of emerging regional trade blocs.

It would provide a non-threatening umbrella for freer trade and investment relations between Australia–New Zealand, Canada, Japan, the European Community, the United States, and some of the emerging newly industrializing countries (NICs). Because there would be no single dominant country in the OECD FTIA, concerns over sovereignty, hegemony, and cultural identity should be muted. And the OECD FTIA would build on the realization that trade diversion becomes less important as the size of an association increases. As Table 7.1 indicates, the OECD FTIA would encompass approximately 60 percent of world trade.

Developing Countries: Possible Objections

The most serious criticism that will be leveled against an OECD FTIA is that it is nothing more than a club for rich countries that has been designed to disadvantage NICs, emerging NICs, and other Third World countries. However loudly proclaimed, this objection is fundamentally wrong.

First, an OECD FTIA would lower barriers (especially nontariff measures) among its members, not raise barriers against outsiders. By far the greatest impact would be the creation of trade among members, not the diversion of trade from the Third World. The creation of trade within the OECD area would promote economic growth in industrial countries and thus attract imports from other countries. The OECD FTIA could reinforce the implicit promise of greater trade with nonmembers through explicit commitments to expand its imports from such countries—not only in total goods but also in "sensitive" products such as apparel and footwear.

Second, the OECD FTIA would have soft boundaries, not hard edges. It would be open to countries that adhere to democratic traditions, pursue market-oriented economic policies, and approach OECD levels of social-welfare legislation (minimum wages, health care, environmental standards, and other benefits). Such entry conditions are necessary to ensure that existing OECD members have a high political and economic "comfort level" with their new partners and vice versa and to provide a strong impetus for the developing nations to "measure up" across a spectrum of social indicators. Such conditions for entry are not impossibly high. After all, both Turkey and Portugal are OECD members. South Korea is expected to be the next new member of the OECD, possibly joining within five years. It is not inconceivable that some Eastern European countries, such as Hungary, would be eligible for membership within a decade.

Third, the OECD FTIA would act as bulwark against sector arrangements that have come to plague the world trading system. Many of these, such as the agreements limiting trade in automobiles, semiconductors, steel, and agriculture, were designed to protect the markets of industrial countries against the products of other industrial countries. In the process, the NICs and the emerging NICs were often hit a glancing blow. If the industrial nations make commitments not to impose barriers against one another, they will be far less likely to impose such barriers against developing countries. And if they make commitments to dismantle existing barriers, it is very likely that developing countries will find that barriers against their own exports will progressively be relaxed.

Practical Steps toward an OECD FTIA
One possible strategy is to announce the concept of an OECD FTIA after the conclusion of the Uruguay Round, perhaps at the Economic Summit of 1991, and to make a political commitment to launch negotiations in 1993, one year after the integration of the European Community. If the implementation began in stages in the mid-1990s, negotiations could be concluded by the year 2000.[2] If this timetable does not work because the European Community is still preoccupied with its own integration, the United States could hold preliminary talks with the Pacific nations. The Pacific talks could focus on Canada, Japan, Australia, and New Zealand but could certainly include aspiring NICs such as Mexico, Korea, and Singapore. Ideas along this line have been floated not only by Secretary of State James Baker (both when he was the secretary of the treasury and in his present position) but also by Senator Bill Bradley (D–N.J.).[3] Once a Pacific group is engaged in negotiations, it might be easier to prompt negotiations in a broader grouping that would include the European Community.

In its early stages, the OECD Free Trade and Investment Area should set itself the task of coordinating the exchange rate policies of its member nations with a view to reducing current account imbalances. This important task represents a modest extension of the goals already adopted by the seven Economic Summit nations. In its later stages, the OECD FTIA should attack all manner of trade and investment barriers. It should reach well beyond the elimination of tariffs and quotas and achieve such goals as the harmonization of technical standards, the uniform protection of intellectual property, open access to government procurement, parallel corporate takeover legislation, similar competition policies, and a comparable corporate tax system.

Such goals are bold, but they are not radical. To a large extent, they have long but informally guided the working agenda of OECD nations. A dramatic statement by the Economic Summit nations of their long-run objectives is now needed to maintain momentum toward economic integration, to soften the edges of emerging regional trade blocs, to arrest the government-sponsored creation of trade cartels, and to forestall the erection of further barriers against foreign investment.

The precise dimensions of an OECD FTIA would depend on progress made in the Uruguay Round, the integration of the European Community, and the evolution of sector arrangements. The features of an OECD FTIA, however, might include the following elements:

- FTIA members would coordinate their exchange rate policies and ultimately their fiscal policies in order to reduce "excessive" current account deficits and surpluses. To some extent, this already represents the goal of the G-7 nations. The commitment to focus policy on current account balances, however, would be made more explicit.

• Quantitative restrictions within the FTIA would be eliminated on a priority basis. Where necessary (as, for example, agricultural trade), quantitative restrictions would be converted to tariffs, and the revenue proceeds thus derived would be allocated to adjustment.

• The principles of national treatment and the right of establishment would govern not only goods but also cross-border investment and trade in services. Work permits and multiple-entry visas would be issued regularly to facilitate the right of establishment.

• Government procurement would be open to member countries on the basis of national treatment. This would apply to both the federal and the subfederal levels of government. A residual exception for military procurement would be limited to military items; for example, offset arrangements would not be permitted for civilian goods and services.

• The mutual recognition approach to technical standards (as now applied within the European Community) would become the norm. In other words, each FTIA member would accept within its markets goods and services produced according to the standards of other members. However, in sensitive areas involving interoperability, public safety, and the environment, the FTIA members would develop common technical standards and testing methods. In time, the members would also develop common patent, copyright, and trademark laws.

• The FTIA members would commit themselves not to grant subsidies unless specifically permitted to do so by means of a "green list." The green list might, for example, permit carefully monitored adjustment subsidies and carefully defined regional subsidies.

• FTIA members would agree to common procedures for handling unfair trade complaints and complaints involving fair but injurious trade. The remedies for such complaints would evolve from remedies designed to limit trade (for example, countervailing duties and voluntary restraint arrangements) to money damage awards and adjustment assistance. FTIA members would also develop dispute settlement procedures with semibinding properties (as in the U.S.-Canada FTA) to oversee the implementation of the agreements.

• FTIA members would eventually develop a common approach to corporate taxation both to alleviate fears about "runaway plants" and to simplify the burdens of the present, very complex system of taxing international income.

• Eventually the members would develop a common approach to competition policy both to harmonize the permitted extent of vertical and horizontal integration and to police the overall FTIA against the creation of monopolies.

• With respect to GATT members that are not parties to the FTIA, there would be specific commitments

  (a) not to erect new barriers;

  (b) to expand the general level of imports, including selected "sensitive" goods such as textiles and apparel, footwear, and carbon steel.

A bold thrust toward the creation of an OECD Free Trade and Investment Area could well provide the trade legacy of the Bush presidency. In the process, growth on a world scale would be invigorated by the force of free markets, and nascent commercial animosity between the regions of the industrial world would be arrested. Working from the principle of "magnetic liberalization," the OECD FTIA could eventually succeed in realizing the goals of free and open trade that have so long inspired and frustrated the GATT.

Tables and Figures

Table 1.1

Projected U.S. Current Account, by Major Component, and Projected Net International Investment Position, 1988–1993 ($ Billions)

	1988	1989	1990	1991	1992	1993
Merchandise trade[a]						
Exports	320	371	426	470	520	570
Imports	447	486	532	570	610	650
Balance	−127	−114	−106	−100	−90	−80
Business and other services: Balance[b]	2	8	13	15	17	19
International investment income: Balance[c]	3	0	−7	−14	−21	−28
Net unilateral transfers and miscellaneous items[d]	−13	−17	−16	−17	−17	−17
Current account balance	−135	−123	−116	−116	−111	−106
Net international investment position[e]	−533	−660	−770	−890	−1,000	−1,100
U.S. assets abroad[f]	1,250	1,350	1,450	1,550	1,650	1,750
Foreign assets in U.S.[f]	1,790	2,010	2,220	2,440	2,650	2,850

Sources: Organization for Economic Cooperation and Development, *OECD Economic Outlook*, June 1989, p. 64 (for 1988, 1989, and 1990 balance-of-payments data). *Wall Street Journal*, June 30, 1989, p. A2 (for 1988 net international investment position, U.S. assets abroad, and foreign assets in U.S.).

Notes:

a. The estimates for 1991–93 assume that the total value of merchandise exports grows by 10 percent per annum from 1990 to 1993, and the total value of merchandise imports grows by 7 percent per annum from 1990 to 1993.

Table 1.1 (continued)

b. The estimates for 1991–93 assume that the balance for business and other services improves by $2 billion each year between 1990 and 1993.

c. The estimates for 1991–93 assume that the net investment income deficit increases each year by 6 percent of the preceding year's current account deficit.

d. For 1988, 1989, and 1990, calculated as the difference between the current account balance and the enumerated entries. For 1991, 1992, and 1993, projected at minus $17 billion per year.

e. The figures are year-end at book value, starting with the recorded values (rounded to the nearest $10 billion) for year-end 1988. The figure for each year, after 1988, was calculated by adding the prior year's current account balance.

f. U.S. assets abroad are assumed to grow $100 billion annually. Foreign assets in the United States are calculated as U.S. assets abroad plus the net international investment position.

Table 2.1
U.S. Merchandise Trade with Selected Countries
and Areas, 1980–1987 ($ Billions)[a]

	Canada[b]	Japan	EC-12[c]	Western Hemisphere Developing Countries[d]	East Asian NICs[e]	OPEC[f]
Exports						
1980	40.3	20.8	58.9	38.7	14.7	17.8
1981	44.6	21.8	57.0	42.1	15.1	21.5
1982	37.9	21.0	52.4	33.6	15.6	22.9
1983	43.3	21.9	48.4	25.7	16.9	16.9
1984	51.8	23.6	50.5	29.7	17.7	14.4
1985	53.3	22.6	49.0	31.0	16.9	12.5
1986	55.5	26.9	53.2	31.1	18.3	10.8
1987	59.8	28.2	60.6	35.0	23.5	11.1
Imports						
1980	42.0	33.0	39.9	38.7	18.8	54.8
1981	46.8	39.9	45.6	40.8	22.1	51.8
1982	46.8	39.9	46.4	39.6	23.8	32.7
1983	52.5	43.6	47.9	43.6	29.6	26.5
1984	66.9	60.4	63.4	50.1	39.1	28.1
1985	69.4	72.4	71.6	49.1	41.9	24.1
1986	68.7	85.5	79.5	44.1	41.1	21.5
1987	71.5	88.1	84.9	49.1	61.3	25.7
Balance						
1980	1.7	−12.2	18.9	0.0	−4.1	−37.0
1981	−2.2	−18.1	11.4	1.3	−7.0	−30.3
1982	−8.9	−19.0	5.9	−6.0	−8.2	−9.9
1983	−9.2	−21.7	0.6	−17.9	−12.6	−9.6
1984	−15.1	−36.8	−12.9	−20.4	−21.4	−13.7
1985	−16.1	−49.7	−22.6	−18.1	−25.0	−11.6
1986	−13.2	−58.6	−26.4	−13.0	−30.8	−10.7
1987	−11.7	−59.8	−24.3	−14.1	−37.7	−14.7

Source: United States Trade Representative, *United States Trade Performance in 1987*, Washington, D.C., 1987, Tables 20–23, 25, 26.

Notes:
    a. Exports valued f.a.s.; imports valued c.i.f.

Table 2.1 (continued)

b. Includes undocumented exports to Canada (about $6.4 billion in 1987).

c. European Community: Belgium, Denmark, Federal Republic of Germany, France, Greece, Ireland, Italy, Luxembourg, the Netherlands, Portugal, Spain, and the United Kingdom.

d. Western Hemisphere Developing Countries: all countries of North and South America (including the Caribbean island nations) except for Canada, Cuba, and the United States.

e. East Asian Newly Industrialized Countries: Hong Kong, Singapore, South Korea, and Taiwan.

f. Organization of Petroleum Exporting Countries: Algeria, Ecuador, Gabon, Indonesia, Iran, Iraq, Kuwait, Libya, Nigeria, Qatar, Saudi Arabia, United Arab Emirates, and Venezuela.

Table 2.2
U.S. Merchandise Trade by Major Product Groups,
1980–1987[a] ($ Billions)

| | Total | Agri-culture | Mineral Fuels | Manufactured Goods[b] | | |
				High Technology	Non-high Technology	Other
Exports						
1980	225.7	41.8	8.2	54.7	106.0	15.1
1981	238.7	43.8	10.3	60.4	111.4	12.8
1982	216.4	37.0	12.8	58.1	97.2	11.4
1983	205.6	36.5	9.6	60.2	88.3	11.1
1984	224.0	30.2	9.5	65.5	98.1	12.7
1985	218.8	29.6	8.2	72.5	107.4	12.1
1986	226.8	26.6	8.2	72.5	107.4	12.1
1987	252.9	29.1	7.8	84.1	116.0	15.9
Imports						
1980	257.0	18.9	82.4	28.0	110.8	17.0
1981	273.4	18.8	84.4	33.8	122.6	13.7
1982	254.9	17.3	67.7	34.6	123.5	11.9
1983	269.9	18.1	60.2	41.4	137.1	13.1
1984	346.4	21.6	63.3	59.5	182.4	19.7
1985	352.5	22.0	55.8	64.8	204.7	15.2
1986	383.0	23.1	39.8	75.1	233.8	11.1
1987	424.1	22.6	46.7	83.5	254.3	17.0
Balance						
1980	–31.3	22.9	–74.2	26.7	–4.7	–1.9
1981	–34.7	25.0	–74.1	26.6	–11.2	–0.9
1982	–38.4	19.7	–54.9	23.6	–26.3	–0.5
1983	–64.2	18.4	–50.6	18.8	–48.7	–2.0
1984	–122.4	16.6	–53.8	6.0	–84.3	–7.0
1985	–133.6	7.6	–45.7	3.6	–105.2	–4.0
1986	–156.1	3.5	–31.7	–2.6	–126.3	0.9
1987	–171.2	6.4	–38.9	0.6	–138.3	–1.1

Source: United States Trade Representative, *United States Trade Performance in 1987*, Washington, D.C., 1987, Tables 4, 14.

Notes:

a. Domestic and foreign exports are valued f.a.s.; general imports are valued c.i.f. The merchandise trade figures in the balance of payments (see Tables 1.1 and 2.3) are valued somewhat differently; in particular, imports are valued f.o.b.

Table 2.2 (continued)

b. High-technology products are defined in the following way (with 1987 export and import figures, in millions of dollars):

	Exports	Imports
Total High Technology	84,071	83,481
Guided missiles, spacecraft	848	48
Communications equipment, electronic components	17,758	36,340
Aircraft and parts	20,968	5,825
Office, computing, accounting machines	19,586	17,918
Ordnance and accessories	654	381
Drugs and medicine	3,258	2,877
Industrial inorganic chemicals	3,641	2,959
Professional and scientific instruments	8,681	11,538
Engines, turbines, parts	3,024	3,739
Plastics and resins	5,654	1,856

Source: United States Trade Representative, *United States Trade Performance in 1987*, Washington, D.C., 1987, Table 15.

Table 2.3
U.S. Current Account, by Major Component, and U.S. Net International Investment Position, 1977–1987 ($ Billions)

	1977	1978	1979	1980	1981	1982
Merchandise Trade:						
Exports	$120.8	$142.1	$184.5	$224.3	$237.1	$211.2
Imports	151.9	176.0	212.0	249.7	265.1	247.6
Balance	–31.1	–33.9	–27.5	–25.5	–28.0	–36.4
Business Services:						
Exports	23.4	27.1	31.2	37.0	42.4	42.3
Imports	20.9	23.7	27.2	29.4	32.3	33.0
Balance	+2.5	+3.4	+4.0	+7.6	+10.2	+9.2
Other Goods and Services:						
Exports	7.9	8.6	7.0	8.7	10.6	12.6
Imports	6.8	8.5	9.5	11.7	12.5	13.7
Balance	+1.1	+0.1	–2.5	–3.0	–1.9	–1.1
International Investment Income:						
Receipts	32.2	42.2	64.1	72.5	86.4	83.5
Payments	14.2	21.7	33.0	42.1	52.3	54.9
Balance	+18.0	+20.6	+31.2	+30.4	+34.1	+28.7

Table 2.3 (continued)

Total Goods and Services:						
Exports	184.3	220.0	286.8	342.5	376.5	349.6
Imports	193.8	229.9	281.7	333.0	362.2	349.3
Balance	-9.5	-9.9	+5.1	+9.5	+14.3	+0.3
Net Unilateral Transfers	-5.0	-5.6	-6.1	-7.6	-7.5	-9.0
Current Account Balance	-14.5	-15.4	-1.0	+1.9	+6.9	-8.7
Net International Investment Position	72.7	76.1	94.5	106.3	141.1	137.0
U.S. Assets Abroad	379.1	447.8	510.6	607.1	719.8	824.9
Foreign Assets in United States	306.4	371.7	416.1	500.8	578.7	688.1

Table 2.3 (continued)

	1983	1984	1985	1986	1987
Merchandise Trade:					
Exports	$201.8	$219.9	$215.9	$224.4	$250.8
Imports	268.9	332.4	338.1	368.7	410.0
Balance	−67.1	−112.5	−122.1	−144.3	−159.2
Business Services:					
Exports	42.3	44.3	45.6	50.7	57.1
Imports	35.8	42.3	45.8	48.2	56.2
Balance	+6.6	+2.0	−0.2	+2.6	+0.9
Other Goods and Services					
Exports	13.0	10.7	9.5	9.5	12.4
Imports	14.2	13.4	13.7	14.3	15.8
Balance	−1.2	−2.7	−4.2	−4.8	−3.4
International Investment Income:					
Receipts	77.3	85.9	88.3	88.2	99.8
Payments	52.4	7.4	62.9	67.4	85.3
Balance	+24.9	+18.5	+25.4	+20.8	14.5

Table 2.3 (continued)

Total Goods and Services:					
Exports	334.4	360.8	359.5	372.8	420.1
Imports	371.2	455.6	460.6	498.5	567.3
Balance	−36.8	−94.8	−101.1	−125.7	−147.2
Net Unilateral Transfers	−9.5	−12.2	−15.3	−15.7	−13.5
Current Account Balance	−46.2	−107.0	−116.4	−141.4	−160.7
Net International Investment Position	89.4	3.5	−110.7	−269.2	−368.2
U.S. Assets Abroad	873.9	896.1	950.3	1,071.4	1,167.8
Foreign Assets in United States	784.5	892.6	1,061.0	1,340.7	1,536.0

Sources: U.S. Department of Commerce, *United States Trade Performance in 1987*, Washington, D.C., June 1988, Table 38; *Statistical Abstract of the United States 1988*, Table 1330; *Survey of Current Business*, June 1988, pp. 77–78.

Table 2.4
Industrial-Country Imports Subject to "Hard-core" Nontariff Measures (NTMs), 1981 and 1986 (Percent)[a]

| | Source of Imports[b] | | | | | |
| | Industrial Countries | | Developing Countries | | All Countries | |
Importer	1981	1986	1981	1986	1981	1986
European Community	10	13	22	23	12	15
Japan	29	29	22	22	25	25
United States	9	15	14	17	11	6
All industrial countries	13	16	9	21	15	18

Sources: World Bank, *World Development Report 1987*, Washington, D.C., 1987, Table 8.3; General Agreement on Tariffs and Trade, *International Trade 1986/87*, Geneva, 1987, Tables A3–A7.

Notes:
a. "Hard-core" NTMs represent a subgroup of all possible NTMs. They are the ones most likely to have significant restrictive effects. Hard-core NTMs include import prohibitions, quantitative restrictions, voluntary export restraints, variable levies, MFA restrictions, and nonautomatic licensing. Examples of other NTMs, which have been excluded, include technical barriers (including health and safety restrictions and standards), minimum pricing regulations, the use of price investigations (for example, for countervailing and antidumping purposes), and price surveillance. The percentage of imports subject to NTMs measures the sum of the value of a country's import group affected by NTMs divided by the total value of its imports of that group.

b. The figures for "all countries" are calculated as weighted averages (1986 weights) of imports originating in industrial and developing countries, respectively. For this calculation, the Eastern trading area is grouped with the developing countries.

Table 2.5
Potential Expansion of Industrial-Country Trade Resulting from the Elimination of Industrial-Country Nontariff Measures[a]

	Export expansion ($ billions)	(percent)	Import expansion ($ billions)	(percent)
European Community	$105	11	$115	12
Japan	$20	8	$30	20
United States	$20	8	$55	13
All industrial countries	$180	10	$260	15

Sources: Gary Clyde Hufbauer, Diane T. Berliner, and Kimberly Ann Elliott, *Trade Protection in the United States: 31 Case Studies* (Washington, D.C.: Institute for International Economics, 1986), Table 1.4; General Agreement on Tariffs and Trade, *International Trade 1987/88*, Geneva, 1988, vol. 2, Tables AA9, AB5, AB8, AB9.

Notes:
a. These are very rough estimates. The starting point is the estimate for U.S. import expansion (13 percent) that would have resulted from the elimination of all special protection prevailing in 1984 as reported in Hufbauer, Berliner, and Elliot, Table 1.4. This percentage was applied to 1987 U.S. imports to derive a figure for potential 1987 import expansion ($55 billion). The import expansion percentages for other countries have been calculated as the ratio between "hard-core" NTMs for those countries and U.S. "hard-core" NTMs in 1986 as reported in Table 2.4, times the U.S. import expansion rate (13 percent). The calculated percentages were applied to each country's 1987 import values to derive figures for its potential 1987 import expansion.

The export expansion estimates have been calculated on the basis of the following expression:

(The subject country's 1987 exports to all industrial countries divided by the total 1987 imports of all industrial countries) times (the ratio between "hard-core" NTMs applied to 1986 industrial-country exports and "hard-core" NTMs applied to 1986 world exports as reported in Table 2.4, namely, 16/18) times (estimated 1987 import expansion for all industrial countries from the elimination of "hard-core" NTMs, namely, $260 billion).

Table 2.6
Potential Expansion of Industrial-Country Trade
Resulting from the Elimination of
Industrial-Country Tariffs[a]

	Export expansion		Import expansion	
	($ billions)	(percent)	($ billions)	(percent)
European Community	$45	4.7	$41	4.5
Japan	$5	2.2	$4	2.4
United States	$8	3.0	$14	3.3
All industrial countries	$75	4.3	$71	4.0

Sources: Alan V. Deardorff and Robert M. Stern, *The Michigan Model of World Production and Trade* (Cambridge, Mass.: MIT Press, 1986) Table 4.6; Central Intelligence Agency, *Handbook of Economic Statistics 1980*, Washington, D.C., 1980, Tables 47, 48; General Agreement on Tariffs and Trade, *International Trade 1987/88*, Geneva, 1988, vol. 2, Tables AA3, AA10.

Notes:
    a. The estimates are based on the data for 1976 reported by Deardorff and Stern, scaled up to 1987 trade levels, assuming that the percentage import and export expansion factors remain constant.

Table 2.7
National Ranking in High Technology
as Assessed by Chief Executives of
More Than 200 Western European Firms

Industry	United States	Japan	West Germany	Scandinavia	United Kingdom	France
Computing	1	2	3	4–5	6	4–5
Electronics	1–2	1–2	3	4	6–7	6–7
Telecommunications	1	2	3	4	5–6	5–6
Biotechnology	1	2	3	4	5	n.a.
Chemicals	1	2	4	4	5	6–7
Metals/alloys	2	1	3	4	5–6	5–6
Engineering	1	2	3	4	5	6
Manufacturing	1–2	1–2	3	4	5	6
Robotics	2	1	3	4	6	5
Mean rank	1.3	1.7	3.0	4.2	5.4	5.8

Source: Wall Street Journal (Europe) and Booz-Allen Hamilton, Management and Technology—A Survey of European Chief Executives, 1984, reprinted in Kenneth Flamm, Targeting the Computer (Washington, D. C.: Brookings Institution, 1987), p. 4.

Table 2.8
International Competitiveness in
High-Technology Industries as Reflected
in Trade Patterns, 1970–1984 (Export-Import Ratios)

	United States	Japan	West Germany	France	United Kingdom	Canada
1970	2.14	2.36	1.69	0.94	1.39	0.65
1971	2.11	2.84	1.72	1.03	1.50	0.69
1972	1.70	3.13	1.77	0.97	1.38	0.65
1973	1.79	3.00	1.88	0.97	1.19	0.58
1974	2.05	2.68	1.89	0.94	1.19	0.52
1975	2.25	3.03	1.62	1.06	1.32	0.54
1976	1.82	3.84	1.65	1.06	1.30	0.64
1977	1.69	4.12	1.59	1.10	1.29	0.63
1978	1.68	4.67	1.62	1.17	1.29	0.72
1979	1.86	3.85	1.53	1.20	1.21	0.71
1980	1.95	4.07	1.48	1.06	1.31	0.72
1981	1.79	4.64	1.38	1.06	1.19	0.72
1982	1.68	4.50	1.47	1.10	1.16	0.78
1983	1.45	4.66	1.38	1.14	1.02	0.73
1984	1.10	5.12	1.41	1.21	1.00	0.74

Source: Peter Morici, *Reassessing American Competitiveness* (Washington, D.C.: National Planning Association, 1988), p. 104.

Table 2.9
Imports of Road Motor Vehicles and Household Appliances, 1980 and 1987 ($ Billions)

	U. S. Imports		Rest of World Imports		World Imports	
	1980	1987	1980	1987	1980	1987
Road motor vehicles	27	73	100	162	127	236
Household appliances	8	21	41	63	48	84
Subtotal	35	95	141	225	175	320
All manufactures	125	318	969	1,417	1,094	1,735
Vehicles and appliances as percent of all manufactures	28.0%	29.9%	14.6%	15.9%	16.0%	18.4%

Sources: General Agreement on Tariffs and Trade, International Trade 1981/82, Geneva, 1982, Tables A19, A24; General Agreement on Tariffs and Trade, International Trade 1987/88, Geneva, 1988, vol. 2, Tables AB3, AB8.

Table 2.10
Causes of the Worsening
Merchandise Trade Deficit, 1980–1988 ($ Billions)

Microeconomic Explanations	–$20
(1) Unfair trade practices:	
New NTMs by industrial countries against U.S. exports	6
New NTMs by the United States against U.S. imports	–17
(2) Lagging U.S. technology	20
(3) Poor U.S. product quality	6
(4) Lower petroleum prices	–35
Macroeconomic Explanations	$114
(1) Dollar exchange rate:	
Rise of 40 index points between 1980 and 1985	120
Fall of 43 index points between 1985 and 1988	–110
(2) Government deficit:	
Increase in unified federal budget deficit from average of $57 billion (2.2 percent of GNP) in FY 1979 and FY 1980 to average of $153 billion (3.2 percent of GNP) in FY 1987 and FY 1988	25
(3) Private savings:	
Decrease in personal savings from 4.9 percent of GNP in 1979 and 1980 to 2.6 percent of GNP in 1987 and 1988	58
(4) Growth gap:	
Lag in ROECD growth of 1 percent per year	9
Decline in U.S. exports to Western Hemisphere developing countries	12
Unexplained residual	$7
Actual deterioration in merchandise trade deficit between 1980 and 1988	$101

Figure 2.1
Exchange Rates of the Dollar, 1981–1988[a]

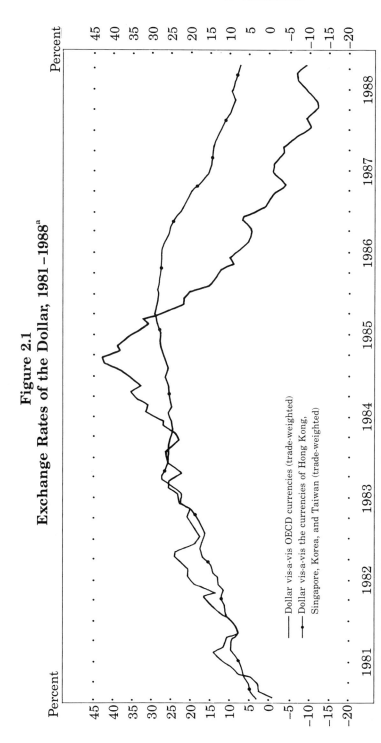

Source: Organization for Economic Cooperation and Development, *OECD Economic Outlook*, December 1988, p. 138.

Note:
a. Percent deviation from the average level prevailing in 1980.

Table 2.11
Index of Exchange Rates of the Dollar, 1980–1989
(1980 = 100)[a]

Year	Index
1980	100.0
1981	109.9
1982	121.1
1983	126.0
1984	135.0
1985	140.3
1986	116.9
1987	103.9
1988	97.2
June 1989	104.8

Sources: Morgan Guaranty Trust Company, *World Financial Markets,* September 1988, p. 16; December 1988, p. 14; June 1989, p. 12; DRI World Service, *International Business and Financial Outlook: Third Quarter 1988,* Lexington, Mass., 1988, p. 42.

Note:
   a. The index is for the nominal value of the dollar against fifteen other industrial-country currencies using bilateral trade weights. For this table, the index has been expressed on a base of 1980 = 100.

Table 2.12

U.S. Gross Savings and Investment, Government Expenditure and Taxes, and Exports and Imports, 1981–1988 ($ Billions)

	1981	1982	1983	1984	1985	1986	1987	1988[a]
(I-S)[b]	-35.0	-109.5	-89.9	-8.7	-22.6	-15.7	47.6	37.7
(G-T)[c]	29.7	110.8	128.5	105.0	132.9	144.4	104.9	87.0
(X-M)[d]	10.6	-1.0	-33.5	-90.9	115.9	-142.4	-160.6	-139.3
Total[e]	5.3	0.0	5.1	5.4	-5.6	-13.6	-8.1	-14.7
Addenda								
I	515.5	447.3	502.3	664.8	641.6	665.9	712.9	760.8
S	550.5	557.1	592.2	673.5	664.2	681.6	665.3	723.2
Federal deficit	63.3	145.9	176.0	169.6	196.0	205.6	157.8	143.0
State and local surplus	34.1	35.1	47.5	65.6	63.1	61.2	52.9	56.0

Sources: Department of Commerce, *Survey of Current Business*, National Income and Products Accounts, Table 5.1, various issues; as summarized by Edward M. Graham, "Trade Deficits, Fiscal Deficits, and the Volatile Dollar," *Marcus Wallenberg Papers on International Finance* 2, no. 3 (1988).

Notes:

a. The 1988 figures are an average of seasonally adjusted, annualized first- and second-quarter results.

b. (I-S) represents gross private investment (I) minus gross private savings (S).

c. (G-T) represents government expenditures (G) by all levels of government (federal, state, local) minus taxes (T) by all levels of government.

d. (X-M) represents exports of goods and services (X) minus imports of goods and services (M), stated on a national income and products account (NIPA) basis (not a balance-of-payments basis).

e. The total equals the statistical discrepancy plus any capital grants received by the United States (for example, an issue of Special Drawing Rights).

Table 2.13
Net Household Savings as a Share of
Disposable Household Income (Percent)

	1975	1976	1977	1978	1979	1980	1981
United States	9.4	7.8	6.7	7.3	7.0	7.3	7.7
Japan	22.8	23.2	21.8	20.8	18.2	17.9	18.3
West Germany	15.1	13.3	12.2	12.0	12.6	12.7	13.5
France	20.2	18.2	18.7	20.4	18.8	17.6	18.0
United Kingdom	12.1	11.6	10.1	11.5	12.6	13.9	12.9
Italy	30.3	29.8	28.2	29.3	29.2	28.0	26.7
Canada	12.7	11.8	11.4	12.6	13.2	13.6	15.4

	1982	1983	1984	1985	1986	1987	1988
United States	7.0	5.5	6.3	4.5	4.2	3.3	4.4
Japan	16.5	16.3	16.0	16.0	16.4	15.1	15.2
West Germany	12.7	10.8	11.4	11.4	12.2	12.3	12.6
France	17.3	15.9	14.5	14.0	13.2	11.5	12.3
United Kingdom	11.9	10.4	10.6	9.8	7.5	5.6	4.1
Italy	25.9	26.1	25.5	24.7	23.7	22.2	22.8
Canada	18.2	14.8	15.0	13.8	11.3	9.7	8.7

Source: OECD Economic Outlook, Paris, June 1989, p. 183.

Figure 2.2
Net National Investment as a Function of
Net National Saving
(Average Annual Percentages of
Gross Domestic Product, 1962–1985)

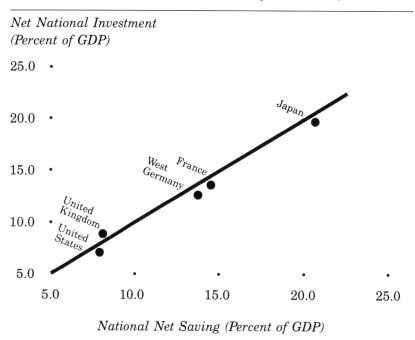

Net National Investment
(Percent of GDP)

National Net Saving (Percent of GDP)

Source: George N. Hatsopoulos, Paul R. Krugman, and Lawrence H. Summers, "U.S. Competitiveness: Beyond the Trade Deficit," *Science,* July 15, 1988, p. 304.

Figure 2.3
Manufacturing Productivity Growth as a Function of
National Net Saving
(Average Annual Percentages, 1962–1985)

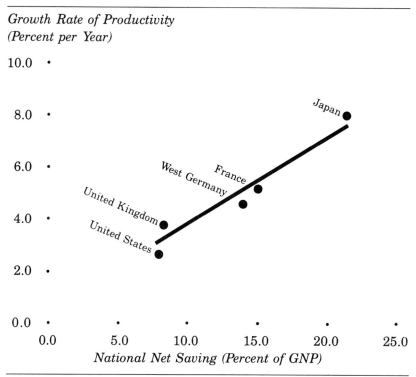

Growth Rate of Productivity
(Percent per Year)

National Net Saving (Percent of GNP)

Source: George N. Hatsopoulos, Paul R. Krugman, and Lawrence H. Summers, "U.S. Competitiveness: Beyond the Trade Deficit," *Science,* July 15, 1988, p. 302.

Table 2.14
Solutions for an Improved
Merchandise Trade Balance, 1988–1993 ($ Billions)

Policy Measures and Trends in Place *as of June 1989*	*$58*
(1) Delayed impact of dollar exchange rate: Fall of 43 index points between 1985 and 1988	19
(2) Offsetting rise of 8 index points in dollar exchange rate between average 1988 and June 1989	–24
(3) Government deficit: Decrease in unified federal budget deficit from average of $153 billion (3.2% of GNP) FY 1987 and FY 1988 to $135 billion (2.1% of GNP) in FY 1993 (CBO baseline forecast)	28
(4) Private savings: Increase in personal savings from 2.6% of GNP in 1987 and 1988 to 4.0% of GNP in 1993	35
New Policy Measures between 1989 and 1993	*$70*
(1) Dollar exchange rate: Further fall of 20 index points from June 1989 level	27
(2) Government deficit: Decrease in federal budget deficit from CBO baseline forecast of $135 billion (2.1% of GNP) in FY 1993 to reduced level of $70 billion (1.1% of GNP) in FY 1993	25
(3) Growth gap: Stimulation of ROECD growth by 1 percent per year ten Debt-relief package for Western Hemisphere developing countries of $20 billion per year	8
Total merchandise *trade balance improvement, 1988 to 1993*	*$128*

Source: See explanations in text.

Table 3.1
Index of World Trade Policy Liberalization,
1960–1988 (Percent per Year)[a]

	1960–1969	1970–1979	1980–1988
Manufactures			
Export volume growth	10.5	7.0	5.0
Output volume growth	7.5	4.5	3.5
Difference	3.0	2.5	1.5
Agriculture			
Export volume growth	4.0	4.5	2.0
Output volume growth	2.5	2.0	2.0
Difference	1.5	2.5	0.0

Source: General Agreement on Tariffs and Trade, *International Trade 1987/88,* Geneva, 1988, vol. 1, Table 1; *International Trade 1988/89,* Geneva, 1989, vol. 1, Table 2.

Note:
   a. The index is the difference between the annual rate of export volume growth and the annual rate of output volume growth.

Figure 3.1
Structure of the Uruguay Round Negotiations:
Recent Trade Levels and Potential for Trade Expansion ($ billions)[a]

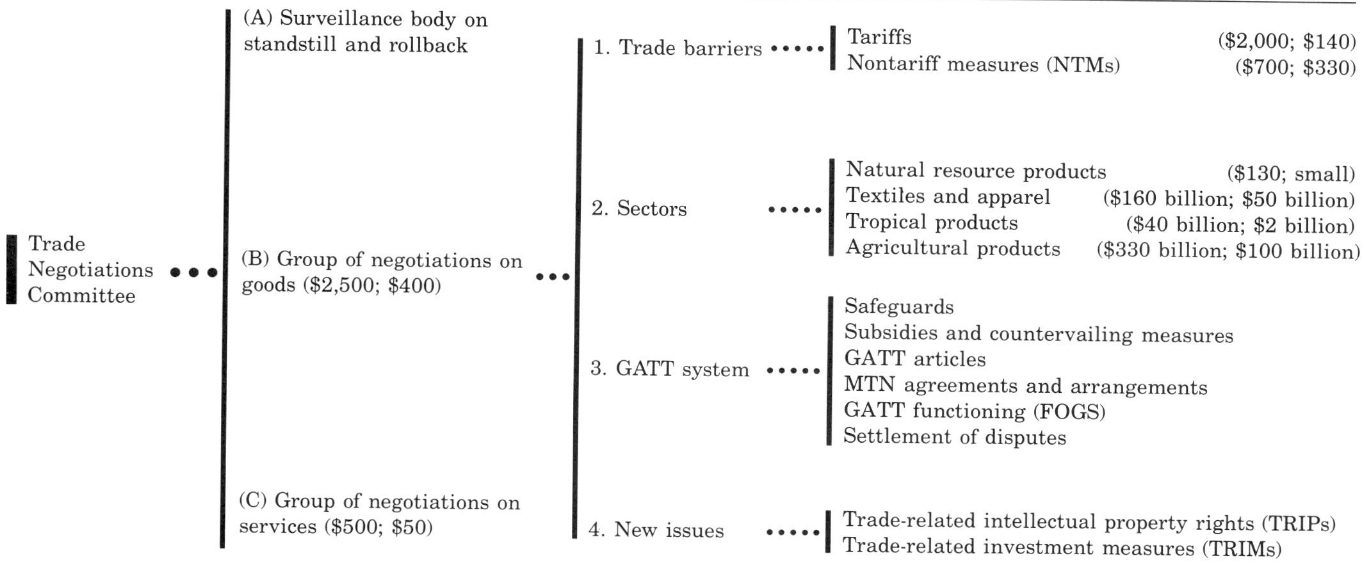

Trade Negotiations Committee

- (A) Surveillance body on standstill and rollback

- (B) Group of negotiations on goods ($2,500; $400)
  - 1. Trade barriers
    - Tariffs ($2,000; $140)
    - Nontariff measures (NTMs) ($700; $330)
  - 2. Sectors
    - Natural resource products ($130; small)
    - Textiles and apparel ($160 billion; $50 billion)
    - Tropical products ($40 billion; $2 billion)
    - Agricultural products ($330 billion; $100 billion)
  - 3. GATT system
    - Safeguards
    - Subsidies and countervailing measures
    - GATT articles
    - MTN agreements and arrangements
    - GATT functioning (FOGS)
    - Settlement of disputes
  - 4. New issues
    - Trade-related intellectual property rights (TRIPs)
    - Trade-related investment measures (TRIMs)

- (C) Group of negotiations on services ($500; $50)

Note:
a. The first figure is world imports, circa 1987. The second figure is a very rough estimate of potential trade expansion from the complete liberalization of restraints. The figures for tariffs and NTMs overlap the figures for particular product categories.

Table 3.2
Cases Involving Countervailing Duties:
Initiating and Subject Countries, 1980–1985
(Cumulative Number of Cases)

Country	Cases initiated	Cases against
United States	252	1
Chile	135	0
Australia	19	2
Canada	11	9
European Community[a]	7	11
Japan	1	2
EEC member states[a]	0	86
Brazil	0	84
Spain	0	39
Argentina	0	30
Mexico	0	28
Peru	0	21
Korea	0	18
New Zealand	0	14
Others (40)	0	80

Source: J. Michael Finger and Julio Nogues, "International Control of Subsidies and Countervailing Duties," *The World Bank Economic Review,* Washington, D.C., September 1987, Table 2.

Note:
   a. EEC member states do not have countervailing duty mechanisms; the countervailing duty instrument exists only at the European Community level. Both member states and the Community have been the objects of countervail investigations conducted by other countries.

Table 4.1
Textile and Apparel Import Penetration Ratios
in Selected Industrial Countries, 1975–1986
(Percent of Consumption)

	United States	Canada	West Germany	United Kingdom	Japan
1975					
Textiles	3.7	27.7	28.1	22.5	6.1
Apparel	9.8	14.8	44.9	27.5	8.3
1981					
Textiles	5.5	25.2	39.4	37.0	7.5
Apparel	18.4	21.1	67.9	44.9	15.3
1986[a]					
Textiles	8.9	28.6	48.5	43.9	10.2
Apparel	30.7	23.3	78.4	45.1	18.6

Sources: Vincent Cable, "Textiles and Clothing in a New Round of Trade Negotiations," *The World Bank Economic Review,* Washington, D.C., September 1987, pp. 628–29; OECD, *Indicators of Industrial Activity,* Paris, vol. 2 (1982), p. 32; vol. 1 (1986), p. 32; General Agreement on Tariffs and Trade, *International Trade 1986/1987,* Geneva, 1987, Tables A30 and A31.

Note:

a. The 1986 penetration ratios were calculated from 1983 ratios, as reported by Cable, by adjusting for import growth and domestic production growth between 1983 and 1986.

Table 4.2
World DRAM Market, 1978–1987 (Percentage Shares)

	1974	1980	1983	1985	1986	1987
United States	100	56	40	22	16	18
Japan	0	40	57	71	80	76
European Community	0	4	3	5	1	1
Rest of world	0	0	0	2	3	5

Source: Financial Times, "World Semiconductor Industry," July 25, 1988, p. 18.

Note:
  a. Percentages are estimates from bar graphs.

Table 4.3
World Semiconductor Market, 1978–1986

	1978	1979	1980	1981	1982	1983	1984	1985	1986
	(billions of dollars)								
U.S.-based shipments	4.78	6.62	8.44	8.00	8.03	9.73	14.00	10.65	11.38
Japan-based shipments	2.49	2.93	3.84	4.17	4.68	6.63	9.80	8.76	11.86
Europe-based shipments	1.41	1.65	1.62	1.54	1.35	1.41	2.10	2.07	2.86
Rest-of-world-based shipments	0.23	0.30	0.32	0.36	0.10	0.14	0.20	0.18	0.25
Total world market	8.91	11.49	14.22	14.07	14.16	17.91	26.10	21.66	26.35
Share of World Market	*(percent)*								
U.S. share	54	58	59	57	57	54	54	49	44
Japanese share	28	25	27	30	33	37	38	40	45
European share	16	14	11	11	10	8	8	10	11
Rest-of-world share	3	3	2	3	1	1	1	1	1
Total world market	100	100	100	100	100	100	100	100	100

Source: Thomas R. Howell et. al., *The Microelectronics Race* (Boulder, Colo.: Westview Press, 1988), Table A.1.

Table 7.1
Trade between Free Trade Areas, 1986 ($ Billions and Shares)

Exporting Area	Importing Area						FTA Subtotal as Share of World Total
	North America	EEC	EFTA	Australia New Zealand	FTA Subtotal	World Total	
North America[a]	107	56	6	7	176	289	0.61
EEC[b]	83	450	85	7	625	789	0.79
EFTA[c]	12	71	19	1	103	133	0.77
Australia and New Zealand	4	4	1	2	11	20	0.55
FTA subtotal	206	581	111	17	915	1,231	0.74
World total	416	746	133	26	1,321	2,119	0.62
FTA subtotal as share of world total	0.50	0.78	0.83	0.65	0.69	0.58	

Sources: General Agreement on Tariffs and Trade, *International Trade 1986/87*, Geneva, 1987, Table A13; International Monetary Fund, *Direction of Trade Statistics, 1988 Yearbook*, Washington, D.C., 1988, pp. 2, 86, 87, 298, 299, 360, 361.

Notes:
   a. Canada and the United States.
   b. Belgium, Denmark, Federal Republic of Germany, France, Greece, Ireland, Italy, Luxembourg, the Netherlands, Portugal, Spain, and the United Kingdom.
   c. Austria, Finland, Iceland, Norway, Sweden, and Switzerland.

Notes

Chapter 1

1. Data from *Economic Report of the President,* January 1989, Tables B-40 and B-60; U.S. Bureau of the Census, *Statistical Abstract of the United States, 1989* (Washington, D.C.: Government Printing Office, 1989), Table 1430; Statement of the U.S. Chamber of Congress to the Republican Platform Committee, August 8, 1988, p. 11.

2. See *Economic Report of the President,* January 1989, Table B-76.

3. The net international investment figure represents the difference between U.S. assets abroad (estimated at $1,254 billion, year-end 1988) and foreign assets in the United States ($1,786 billion, year-end 1988). See *Survey of Current Business,* June 1989.

See Table 2.3 for past data (1977-87) and Table 1.1 for forecasts (1988-93) of the U.S. balance of payments and the U.S. net international investment position. Net international investment figures stated at book value greatly overstate the U.S. net debtor position by comparison with figures stated at market values. In terms of market value, the United States probably was a net debtor to the extent of less than $100 billion in 1988. Whether measured at book value or at market value, however, the U.S. net investment position deteriorated by about $600 billion between 1980 and 1988.

4. It is no accident that the deterioration in the U.S. net international investment position ($639 billion) was practically the same as the accumulated merchandise deficits ($797 billion) minus accumulated international investment income ($166

189

billion) during the Reagan years. The year-to-year change in the net international investment position approximately equals the current account balance during the year. In turn, the current account balance approximately equals the sum of the merchandise trade balance and the investment income balance. For a precise reconciliation of current account balances and changes in the net international investment position, see *Survey of Current Business,* June 1988, p. 77.

5. I refer to the merchandise trade deficit rather than the more comprehensive (but less familiar) current account deficit. In terms of political arithmetic, the merchandise trade deficit is the more pressing problem. Tables 2.3 and 1.1 show the relation between the merchandise trade deficit (about $127 billion in 1988) and the current account deficit (about $135 billion in 1988).

6. Quoted in *The New York Times,* October 9, 1988, p. E4. A sophisticated body of opinion holds that too much is made of trade deficits and capital inflows. According to this view, the United States should not be concerned if it buys $90 billion of imports from Japan and sells only $30 billion of exports to Japan; nor should Americans be worried if Japanese investors buy half of downtown Los Angeles. Although the merits of these ideas promise good debate in academic circles, the "sophisticated" view strikes most Americans as naive and complacent. This view has been expressed in the editorial pages of *The Wall Street Journal* (e.g., the essays by Herbert Stein, "Leave the Trade Deficit Alone," March 11, 1987, and Mieczyslaw Karczmar, "Trade-Deficit Truths: Not to Worry," October 20, 1988).

7. The erosion of the "free-trade coalition" by the force of trade deficits was noted in *The Wall Street Journal,* October 16, 1985, p. 1. Despite this erosion, it should be stressed that there have been several liberal trade initiatives in the 1980s: the Caribbean Basin Initiative, the U.S.-Israel Free Trade Agreement, the Semiconductor Tariff Agreement, renewal of the Generalized System of Preferences, the launching of the Uruguay Round, and the U.S.-Canada Free Trade Agreement.

8. Eventually, the Reagan administration extended or enlarged case-by-case protection to include several important in-

dustries: automobiles, motorcycles, steel, textiles and apparel, lumber, semiconductors, and machine tools. See Gary Hufbauer, Diane Berliner, and Kimberly Ann Elliott, *Trade Protection in the United States: 31 Case Studies* (Washington, D.C.: Institute for International Economics, 1986). Nevertheless, throughout his tenure in office, President Reagan remained an adamant free trader. In his last presidential broadcast from his Santa Barbara ranch, Reagan denounced protectionism as "a cheap form of nationalism" and reminisced: "[In 1932], when I cast my first ballot for president, I voted for Franklin Delano Roosevelt, who opposed protectionism and called for the repeal of that disastrous tariff [the Smoot-Hawley Tariff Act of 1930]." See *The Washington Post,* November 27, 1988, p. A13.

9. As the financial inflows associated with the merchandise trade deficits continue in the 1990s, Congress will likely take up the debate over inward foreign investment. See John Kline, "Trade Act of 1988: Investment Issues for the Bush Administration," *The Marcus Wallenberg Papers on International Finance,* no. 5 (International Law Institute, 1989).

10. Between May 1986 and May 1987, during a period of tough trade disputes, the percentage of Japanese who regard the United States as an unfriendly country jumped from 31 percent to 50 percent. In the October 1988 Olympic Games, Korean audiences cheered not only good plays by Soviet athletes but also bad plays by American athletes. Noting such reactions, on April 10, 1989, a group of thirty-three prominent American economists, led by Jagdish Bhagwati of Columbia University, issued a statement criticizing the growing trend toward managed trade and retaliatory measures. Confronting weak countries, the statement says, thrusts the United States in the role of bully, while confronting strong countries, such as the European Community, often produces a "spirited reaction." The economists deplore "quantity-oriented" trade arrangements as undermining the "rule-oriented" regime of the General Agreement on Tariffs and Trade (GATT).

11. Chapter 2 examines the impact of unfair trade practices on trade flows. For a discussion of adjustment issues, see Gary Hufbauer and Howard F. Rosen, *Trade Policy for Troubled Industries* (Washington, D.C.: Institute for International Econom-

ics, 1986); Robert Z. Lawrence and Robert E. Litan, *Saving Free Trade* (Washington, D.C.: Brookings Institution, 1986).

12. The twenty-four member states of the Organization for Economic Cooperation and Development are Australia, Austria, Belgium, Canada, Denmark, Finland, France, the Federal Republic of Germany, Greece, Iceland, Ireland, Italy, Japan, Luxembourg, the Netherlands, New Zealand, Norway, Portugal, Spain, Sweden, Switzerland, Turkey, the United Kingdom, and the United States.

The OECD Free Trade and Investment Area (FTIA) should be open to non-OECD countries that adhere to democratic traditions, pursue market-oriented economic policies, and approach OECD levels of social-welfare legislation (minimum wages, health care, environmental standards, and so on). These entry conditions are designed to ensure that OECD members have a high political and economic "comfort level" with their new partners and vice versa. The alternative to a high comfort level is the continuance of trade and investment barriers.

13. In fact, some of the long-term goals might be achieved sooner than the elimination of quotas and investment barriers.

14. See Alfred Reifman, "A Survey of U.S. International Economic Policy and Problems," Congressional Research Service, Washington, D.C., October 17, 1988, chap. 2.

15. See Gregory F. Treverton, "The Next American President and the Alliance," *Critical Issues* (Council on Foreign Relations, New York) 8 (1988).

16. See Henry Kissinger, "The Challenge of a 'European Home,' " *The Washington Post,* December 4, 1988, p. L7.

17. This was one of the arguments behind the call by Congressman Richard Gephardt, after the November 1988 election, for a U.S.-European Community trade accord.

18. Congressional power to regulate foreign commerce is enumerated in Article 1, Section 8, of the Constitution.

19. See I. M. Destler, *American Trade Politics* (Washington, D.C., and New York: Institute for International Economics and Twentieth Century Fund, 1986).

20. From its creation in 1916, the U.S. Tariff Commission has proved more attentive to congressional concerns than presidential wishes. In the Trade Act of 1974, the U.S. Tariff Commis-

sion was named the U.S. International Trade Commission and given additional responsibilities.

21. For a "side-by-side" comparison between the Omnibus Trade and Competitiveness Act of 1988 (H.R. 4848) and preceding law, see Bureau of National Affairs, *International Trade Reporter*, August 10, 1988. For nonlegal summaries of the 1988 act, see U.S. Chamber of Commerce, *The Omnibus Trade and Competitiveness Act of 1988* (Washington, D.C., 1988); see also Coudert Brothers, "Major Developments in U.S. Trade Law: Ten Sectors of the Omnibus Trade and Competitiveness Act of 1988," Washington, D.C., 1988.

22. After May 31, 1991, the president must request an extension of fast-track negotiating authority to May 31, 1993; the extension will be granted automatically unless the House or the Senate objects.

23. In the original Gephardt amendment a formula approach would have been used to restrict U.S. imports from countries that persist in maintaining large trade surpluses and unfair trade practices. "Super 301" merely requires the U.S. trade representative to give "priority" attention to such countries. See Raymond J. Ahearn and Alfred Reifman, "Trade Legislation in 1987: Congress Takes Charge," in *Issues in the Uruguay Round,* ed. Robert E. Baldwin and J. David Richardson (Cambridge, Mass.: NBER, 1988). Despite this moderation, Congress placed somewhat more emphasis on sticks than on carrots. A major thrust of the 1988 trade act was to shift the priority of U.S. trade policy toward unilateral action. See I. M. Destler, "United States Trade Policymaking in the Uruguay Round," in *Domestic Trade Politics and the Uruguay Round,* ed. Henry R. Nau (New York: Columbia University Press, New York, 1989), pp. 191-207.

Chapter 2

1. See, for example, the gloomy prognoses offered by *The Economist,* "World Economy Survey," September 24, 1988; David D. Hale, "The Dollar Rally of 1988," Kemper Financial Services, Chicago, July 1988; and C. Fred Bergsten, *America in the World Economy: A Strategy for the 1990s* (Washington, D.C.: Institute for International Economics, 1988).

2. As a result of federal budget deficits between 1980 and 1988, the federal debt held by the public (including foreigners) grew from 26 percent of Gross National Product to 421 percent of GNP, and interest payments grew from 8.9 percent of federal budget outlays to 14.3 percent. See *Economic Report of the President,* January 1989, Tables B-1, B-76, and B-77. For these calculations, federal outlays include both on-budget and off-budget expenditures.

3. For Gramm-Rudman-Hollings (GRH) targets and Congressional Budget Office (CBO) forecasts, see *OECD Economic Outlook,* June 1989, p. 62. The calculations in this paragraph assume a nominal Gross National Product in 1993 of $6,400 billion (representing about 7 percent annual nominal growth, comprised of 2-3 percent real growth and 4-5 percent inflation). It should be noted that both the GRH targets and the CBO forecasts are stated in terms of the unified budget, which includes the surplus in Social Security trust funds. The calculations also assume that about 78 percent of newly issued federal debt ends up as debt held by the public.

4. By comparison, the total external debt of all developing countries at the end of 1989 will be about $1,300 billion. See International Monetary Fund, *World Economic Outlook,* Washington, D.C., October 1988, Table A46. At market values, taking into account prevailing secondary market discounts, the debt figure of less developed countries probably will not exceed $700 billion.

5. See *Economic Report of the President,* January 1989, Table B1. In the 1970s, the current account surplus averaged 0.8 percent of Gross National Product; in the 1980s, the current account deficit averaged 1 percent of Gross National Product. In other words, the reversal of the current account balance (and the corresponding reversal of capital flows) between the 1970s and the 1980s averaged 1.8 percent of GNP. If this reversal of capital flows had financed the creation of productive assets in the United States, and if all other things had remained equal, then gross fixed nonresidential investment would have increased from 10.8 percent of GNP in the 1970s to about 12.6 percent in the 1980s (10.8 percent plus 1.8 percent equals 12.6 percent). Instead, nonresidential investment barely changed.

6. Total reproducible assets are typically about three times

GNP. For this calculation, assets are measured as the net stock of reproducible tangible wealth (in other words, making allowance for depreciation and excluding the value of land and intellectual property). See *Survey of Current Business,* October 1988, pp. 35-36. In some asset categories, of course, the concentration of foreign ownership is much higher than the projected average *net* foreign ownership figure of about 6 percent. For example, more than a quarter of downtown commercial real estate in New York, Los Angeles, Washington, Houston, and some other cities is foreign owned, primarily by Japanese investors. See Martin Tolchin and Susan Tolchin, *Buying into America* (New York: Time Books, 1988).

7. The figure of $13,200 billion for nominal GNP represents a compound rate of growth of about 7 percent per year in nominal terms.

8. In this calculation, no account has been taken of errors and omissions in the U.S. balance of payments. Marris argues that, even though world payments and receipts regularly show a world current account deficit (a logical impossibility), it is very likely that the U.S. current account deficit has not been consistently overstated. Instead, it is more likely that the European current account surplus has been consistently and substantially understated. See Stephen Marris, *Deficits and the Dollar* (Washington, D.C.: Institute for International Economics, 1987), pp. 300-302.

9. By a process of elimination, virtually all the improvements in current accounts must come from the merchandise trade balance. If the United States is to retain its status as a creditworthy nation, investment income must be paid; and the other accounts (nonfactor services and unilateral transfers) are probably too small to allow much scope for improvement. Moreover, the decisive factor in the merchandise trade balance is manufactures. "Even if the U.S. could return to a $20 billion agricultural surplus and eliminate all the remaining petroleum deficit, the improvement in our total trade balance would affect less than half of the 1987 level of the manufactures trade deficit." (Stephen Cooney, *New Directions for U.S. Trade: Manufacturing Is the Key to Eliminating the Trade Deficit,* Report by the National Association of Manufacturers, Washington, D.C., December 1988, p. 12.)

10. For a compendium of unfair foreign practices, see United States Trade Representative, *1989 National Trade Estimate Report on Foreign Trade Barriers,* Washington, D.C., 1989. For a detailed indictment of Japanese trade policy, see Clyde V. Prestowitz, Jr., *Trading Places: How We Allowed Japan to Take the Lead* (New York: Basic Books, 1988). For a more balanced critique of Japan, see Bela Balassa and Marcus Noland, *Japan in the World Economy* (Washington, D.C.: Institute for International Economics, 1988). Gephardt now acknowledges that, at most, some 20 percent of the trade deficit is attributable to unfair foreign trade practices. See *The Washington Post,* April 30, 1989, p. H8. Other observers, such as William Cline at the Institute for International Economics, put the figure at 10 to 15 percent.

11. These figures are calculated as the proportionate increase in the trade coverage of nontariff measures (NTMs) (see Table 2.4) times the projected amount of export or import expansion resulting from the total elimination of all "hard-core" NTMs (see Table 2.5). The actual calculation is $4 billion for U.S. exports; an estimate of $6 billion probably overstates the impact of NTMs on U.S. exports.

12. In fact, trade negotiations have long been viewed not as a means to improve one nation's trade balance but as a means of "leveling the playing field," removing anticompetitive barriers, enhancing productivity, and lowering prices. Elsewhere it has been argued that the pace at which trade liberalization measures are implemented might be partly scaled to the extent of a country's trade surplus (faster pace) or trade deficit (slower pace). See Gary Clyde Hufbauer and Jeffrey J. Schott, *Trading for Growth: The Next Round of Trade Negotiations* (Washington, D.C.: Institute for International Economics, 1985), pp. 22-23; and Gary Clyde Hufbauer, "Should Unconditional MFN be Revived, Retired, or Recast?" in *Issues in World Trade Policy,* ed. Richard Snape (London: Macmillan Press, 1986).

13. Almost weekly, articles appear about lagging U.S. technology. For example, "The Global Biotechnology Race," *The New York Times,* July 13, 1988, p. D1; "U.S. Lags in Television Research," *Journal of Commerce,* October 27, 1988, p. 5A; *The Wall Street Journal Reports,* "Technology," November 14, 1988.

Closely related are accounts of poor U.S. productivity performance. See, for example, *Business Week,* "The Productivity Paradox," June 6, 1988; The MIT Commission on Industrial Productivity, *Made in America: Regaining the Productive Edge* (Cambridge, Mass.: MIT Press, 1989).

14. Between 1980 and 1987, U.S. high-tech exports grew by 56 percent and world high-tech exports grew by 80 percent. The modest shortfall of U.S. high-tech exports from world norms can easily be attributed to the strong dollar. For this comparison, high-tech products are defined as chemicals and office and telecommunications equipment. See General Agreement on Tariffs and Trade, *International Trade 1987/88,* vol. 2, Geneva, 1988, Tables AB1 and AB8; *International Trade 1983/84,* Geneva, 1984, Table A23.

15. The estimate of $20 billion may be exaggerated because U.S. markets for high-tech products grew faster than U.S. markets for non-high-tech manufactures. Thus, quite apart from any lag in U.S. technological capability, the scope for high-tech imports was larger.

16. The Chrysler Corporation recently ran a two-page advertisement featuring Lee Iacocca sympathizing with American complaints about automobile quality. See *The Wall Street Journal,* October 31, 1988, pp. B8-B9. A Gallup Organization survey showed that American consumers say they are willing to pay substantially higher prices for better quality (for example: high-quality automobiles, $14,518, average-quality automobiles, $12,000; high-quality televisions, $500, average-quality televisions, $300). In response to such findings and the obvious penetration of the consumer goods market by imports, U.S. firms are placing much greater emphasis on quality. See *The Washington Post,* October 2, 1988, p. A2. In this respect, U.S. firms are beginning to emulate West German firms long known for their high-quality products and good after-purchase service. See *The New York Times,* October 6, 1988, p. D1.

17. International Monetary Fund, *International Financial Statistics, 1988 Yearbook,* Washington, D.C., 1988; and *International Financial Statistics, October 1988,* Washington, D.C., 1988. The price decline continued in 1988. In real terms, adjusted for inflation, oil prices have now returned to the level that pre-

vailed prior to the 1973 oil shock. See *The Economist,* October 15, 1988, p. 81.

18. See, generally, Bergsten, *America in the World Economy.*

19. This summary glosses over the famous "J-curve." For a short time after a dollar appreciation, the trade balance actually improves before the higher dollar price of exports and the lower dollar price of imports are offset by changes in the quantity of imports and the quantity of exports. Conversely, for a short time after a dollar depreciation, the trade balance actually worsens.

20. See, for example, Marris, *Deficits and the Dollar;* and Ralph C. Bryant et al., *Empirical Macroeconomics for International Economics* (Washington, D.C.: Brookings Institution, 1988); William R. Cline, *American Trade Adjustment: The Global Impact* (Washington, D.C.: Institute for International Economics, March 1989).

21. The Louvre Accord was a cooperative effort by the seven Economic Summit Nations (the Group of Seven) to end the dollar fall and stabilize currency relationships at levels prevailing in early 1987. Since then, the G-7 nations have followed a secret target-zone system in managing exchange rates. See Yoichi Funabashi, *Managing the Dollar: From the Plaza to the Louvre* (Washington, D.C.: Institute for International Economics, 1988). (The target-zone system was propounded by John Williamson, *The Exchange Rate System* [Washington, D.C.: Institute for International Economics, 1985].) The current secret range for the dollar is thought to be 120 to 140 yen and 1.60 to 1.90 marks. See *The Wall Street Journal,* November 14, 1988, p. A8. This range was severely tested by the strong dollar in May and June 1989.

22. In "normal" times a 20 percent fall in the dollar might increase U.S. inflation by about 4 to 5 percent over its baseline path after four to five years. See Bryant et al., *Empirical Macroeconomics for International Economies,* Simulation F. However, the inflationary danger is mitigated by a sluggish economy.

23. This calculation assumes that the first 8 index points of dollar depreciation merely take the dollar back to its 1988 average level of 97 (see Table 2.11). The next 9 index points represent further depreciation (below the 1988 level of the dollar). Calculated at $3 billion trade improvement for each index point, the ensuing improvement would be $27 billion.

24. There are a great many techniques of policy intervention, ranging from official pronouncements to press leaks to exchange-market intervention to interest rate changes. All these have been used by James Brady and Alan Greenspan since April 1989.

25. The prescriptions of target-zone advocates for controlling current account imbalances are set forth by John Williamson and Marcus H. Miller, *Targets and Indicators: A Blueprint for the International Coordination of Economic Policy* (Washington, D.C.: Institute for International Economics, September 1987). Broadly speaking, Williamson and Miller recommend the use of monetary policy to adjust exchange rates and the use of fiscal policy to manage domestic demand.

26. See Robert Barro, "The Ricardian Approach to Budget Deficits," NBER Working Paper 2685, Cambridge, Mass., August 1988; *The Economist,* December 10, 1988, p. 69.

27. See *OECD Economic Outlook,* Paris, June 1988, pp. 101-6; and December 1988, pp. 88-92; *The Economist,* September 17, 1988, p. 75. The difference between GDP and GNP is that GDP excludes net investment income received from abroad.

28. A larger government deficit worsens the trade balance *directly* by prompting the domestic absorption of more goods and services; it can also worsen the trade balance *indirectly* by leading to higher interest rates and therefore an appreciation of the exchange rate. Here we are concerned only with the direct impact.

29. See Bryant et al., *Empirical Macroeconomics for Interdependent Economies,* Simulation C. The implication of this estimate is that a 1 percent reduction in the fiscal deficit will also diminish the private sector financial surplus (private savings minus private investment) by about $25 billion—for example, by stimulating private investment through lower interest rates.

30. Most of the projected improvement can be attributed to rapidly rising Social Security trust funds. In fiscal 1988 the "on-budget" deficit of $194 billion was offset by a Social Security surplus of $39 billion, leaving a unified deficit of $155 billion; in fiscal 1993, the "on-budget" deficit of $238 billion will be offset by a Social Security surplus of $103 billion, leaving a

unified deficit of about $135 billion. See *OECD Economic Outlook,* Paris, June 1989, p. 62.

31. Before the election, Herbert Stein, like many economists, made light of such antitax declarations: "The main plank in Mr. Bush's economic platform is his promise that he will never raise taxes. This is like a small boy's declaration that he will never go to the dentist again—sincerely meant but of little predictive value." See *The New York Times,* September 4, 1988, p. F5.

32. A pay-as-you-go-at-the-margin principle is especially important now because the discovery of growing surpluses in the Social Security trust fund will greatly increase the temptation to add federal spending programs without finding new revenue sources. See Lawrence J. Haas, "Paying as You Go," *National Journal,* October 23, 1988.

33. After the election, Bush said that he would define narrowly what constitutes a "tax." Thus, the catastrophic health care premium is not considered a tax. In a similar spirit, loophole-closing measures are not considered a "new tax." See *Tax Notes,* November 14, 1988, p. 688.

34. Data on personal savings are reported in *Economic Report of the President,* Washington, D.C., January 1989, Table B28; and *Survey of Current Business,* September 1989, p. 7. The coefficient of the change of $25 billion per 1 percent of GNP in household savings is based on Bryant et al., *Empirical Macroeconomics for Interdependent Economies,* Simulation C.

35. Irrespective of fortuitous events, President Bush and the Congress should encourage personal savings through policy measures. For example, tax burdens could be adjusted so that they fall more heavily on current consumption and less heavily on savings (keeping total taxes constant). Specifically, a lower capital gains tax could be partly financed through an end to public subsidies for private mansions by placing a cap of, say, $40,000 on mortgage interest deductions that can be claimed by any one family. Summers has suggested three other ways to raise private savings: (1) remove Social Security trust funds from the budget, so that Congress will pay more attention to the deficit; (2) devote presidential rhetoric to private savings; (3) restore Individual Retirement Accounts. See Lawrence H.

Summers, "The Budget Deficit Problem: 1989," *Tax Notes,* March 6, 1989, pp. 1249-56.

36. See *The Washington Post,* October 1, 1988, p. E1.

37. *OECD Economic Outlook,* Paris, June 1988, Tables 1 and R1.

38. This calculation assumes that 1 percent faster growth in the ROECD nations improves the U.S. trade balance by $10 billion. See Bryant et al., *Empirical Macroeconomics for Interdependent Economies,* Simulation G.

39. In 1980, when world merchandise imports were $1,928 billion, imports by Western Hemisphere developing countries were $111 billion. In 1987, when world imports were $2,418 billion, imports by Western Hemisphere developing countries were only $110 billion. If the Western Hemisphere developing countries had maintained their share of world merchandise imports, their imports would have been $29 billion higher, and U.S. exports to the region would plausibly have increased by $12 billion (40 percent of the counterfactual increase). Data are from International Monetary Fund, *Direction of Trade Statistics, Yearbook 1986,* Washington, D.C., 1986, and *Yearbook 1988,* Washington, D.C., 1988.

40. See Richard E. Feinberg, "How to Reverse the Defunding of Latin America by the Multilateral Lending Agencies," Overseas Development Council, Washington, D.C., September 15, 1988.

41. Microeconomic events will surely affect the trade balance between 1988 and 1993, but collectively their effect is unlikely to exceed $20 billion one way or the other.

Chapter 3

1. The standard work on the General Agreement on Tariffs and Trade (GATT) is Kenneth W. Dam, *The GATT: Law and International Economic Organization* (Chicago: University of Chicago Press, 1970). For a current overview, see Jeffrey J. Schott, "U.S. Policies Toward the GATT: Past, Present and Prospective" (unpublished manuscript, Institute for International Economics, Washington, D.C., October 1988).

2. These disciplines are especially valued by small- and medium-sized GATT members—countries that are not in a

strong position to defend their trade interests in bilateral negotiations with the European Community (EC), Japan, or the United States. About thirty to forty small GATT members have formed the "de la Paix" group, which meets monthly or so at the Hotel de la Paix in Geneva to coordinate the defense of multilateral principles in the Uruguay Round.

3. See John H. Jackson and William J. Davey, *Legal Problems of International Economic Relations* (St. Paul: West Publishing, 1986), p. 9. Between the Smoot-Hawley Tariff of 1930 and the initial implementation of the GATT in 1947, the United States cut its average tariff on dutiable imports from 53 percent to 13 percent under the auspices of the Reciprocal Trade Agreements program.

4. See Gary Clyde Hufbauer, "The International Economy to 1999: Anticipations of the Marcus Wallenberg Centennial," *The Marcus Wallenberg Papers on International Finance* 1, no. 1 (International Law Institute, 1986). Data on GNP growth rates come primarily from OECD sources, for example, *OECD Economic Outlook,* Paris, June 1988.

5. The explicit assumption underlying this index is that, even without trade liberalization, exports would grow by the same rate as output because both the demand for imports and the supply of exports would grow by roughly the rate of output growth. Trade liberalization permits exports to grow faster than output. (The implicit assumption is that neither output growth nor demand growth is biased in favor of import substitutes or in favor of exports on a global basis.) For the latest data, see GATT, *International Trade 1988/89,* vol. 1, Geneva, 1989, Table 2.

6. See Alan V. Deardorff and Robert M. Stern, *The Michigan Model of World Production and Trade* (Cambridge, Mass.: MIT Press, 1986), Table 4.4.

7. GATT is a beleaguered institution for several reasons: its diminished ability to cut trade barriers, its procedural difficulties in adjudicating or settling trade complaints, the proliferation of competing (and sometimes inconsistent) sectoral arrangements and free trade areas, and the tendency of large countries to negotiate their trade problems outside of GATT.

For an eloquent exposition of the importance of the Uruguay Round, see C. Michael Aho and Jonathan David Aronson, *Trade*

Talks: America Better Listen! (New York: Council on Foreign Relations, 1985).

For a quantitative review of trade policy, see Margaret Kelly et al., "Issues and Developments in International Trade Policy," *Occasional Paper 63,* International Monetary Fund, Washington, D.C., December 1988.

8. Much of the pre-Montreal description is adapted, with permission, from Ashok Desai, "India and the Uruguay Round," Conference on the Multilateral Trade Negotiations and the Developing Countries, Washington, D.C., September 15-16, 1988. Other sources include General Agreement on Tariffs and Trade, *News of the Uruguay Round,* various issues; *Inside U.S. Trade,* Special Report, September 30, 1988, and Special Report, December 12, 1988; and various press reports. For a skeptical note on the outcome of the April 1989 meeting, see the remarks of former Ambassador Michael Smith, reported in *Inside U.S. Trade,* April 28, 1989, p. 1. For a survey of the potential gains to recalcitrant developing countries from participating in the round, see Bela Balassa, "Interest of Developing Countries in the Uruguay Round," *The World Economy,* March 1988. For an overall review, see Sidney Golt, *The GATT Negotiations 1986-1990: Origins, Issues and Prospects* (London: British-North American Committee, 1988); and John Whalley, ed., *The Uruguay Round and Beyond* (London: Macmillan, 1989).

9. "Gray area" is another phrase to describe trade measures that violate the spirit but not necessarily the letter of GATT.

10. In fact, the United States has characterized the European Community offer as having "little economic meaning." See *Inside U.S. Trade,* Special Report, September 30, 1988, p. 41.

11. Australia and New Zealand have also retained high tariffs, but both countries are in the process of reducing them quite apart from the Uruguay Round. By 1993, for example, the top Australian tariff will be 15 percent.

12. A country that "binds" its tariffs or other trade policy instruments in GATT makes a commitment to all GATT members not to make that instrument more restrictive. If the country later violates its commitment, it is obligated to pay compensation to all GATT members. In past GATT rounds a number of countries granted tariff concessions but did not bind them in

GATT; accordingly, those tariffs could be raised later simply by renegotiating them with the principal suppliers.

13. See World Bank, *World Development Report 1987,* Washington, D.C., 1987, p. 138.

14. This calculation is made as follows: a 50 percent tariff cut might average 15 percentage points; in 1987, developing-country imports were about $480 billion; assuming a unit elasticity of demand, each percentage point of a tariff cut might increase the value of developing-country imports by about $4.8 billion annually, and a 15 percentage point cut would increase the overall value of imports by about $70 billion. On the whole, developing countries must pay for their imports with larger exports; hence, after the necessary exchange rate devaluations and internal economic rationalizations, developing-country exports would also rise. The induced export expansion, however, has not been counted in the $70 billion estimate of world trade expansion.

15. The seven countries are Canada, Australia, Hong Kong, Hungary, South Korea, New Zealand, and Switzerland. More recently, the European Community and Japan have also proposed tariff-cutting formulas. See *Inside U.S. Trade,* August 4, 1989, p. 1.

16. In request-and-offer bargaining, one country requests concessions from the countries that constitute its principal markets and offers concessions to its principal suppliers. At the end of the day, concessions are leveled up or down to minimize the "free-rider" problem—the demoralizing effect that occurs when some countries do not make as many concessions as they receive in the round-robin of bilateral bargaining.

It is worth noting that four key senators who have ties to the U.S. textile industry have publicly opposed formula tariff cuts. See *Inside U.S. Trade,* November 11, 1988, p. 6. For a description of the U.S. approach, combining tariff and nontariff measures (NTMs) in the same talks, see *Inside U.S. Trade,* June 16, 1989, p. 4.

17. This figure is calculated as 15 percent of 1987 developing-country imports of $480 billion (the 15 percent is based on the estimate of the potential expansion in the imports of the industrial countries, reported in Table 2.5). Again, as with tariff

cuts, if developing-country imports grow by $70 billion annually owing to the elimination of NTMs, developing-country exports would also need to grow through economic restructuring and rationalization.

18. In earlier GATT rounds, tariff reductions were achieved because there was a common will to forge an agreement, and quibbling about what constitutes a tariff did not occur. Today the common will to dismantle nontariff measures is weak, and the debate over the definition of nontariff measures has correspondingly been endless.

19. Preshipment inspection is used to certify, for example, that red meat satisfies the health standards of the importing country. Rules of origin are used to determine whether, for example, apparel shipped to Western Europe from Canada is in fact "Canadian" rather than "Chinese."

20. Natural resource goods include fish, forestry products, iron ore, and nonferrous minerals; the United States would like to expand the coverage to include energy products. The trade figures cited for the year 1987 are from General Agreement on Tariffs and Trade, *International Trade 1987/88*, vol. 2, Geneva, 1988, Table AB3. For this calculation, natural resource goods are taken to include "raw materials" and "ores and minerals."

21. See ibid.

22. U.S. imports might rise by $15 billion, and ROECD imports might rise by the same amount on a per capita basis, or about a total of $35 billion. These estimates are based on William R. Cline, *The Future of World Trade in Textiles and Apparel* (Washington, D.C.: Institute for International Economics, 1987), Table 8.1.

23. "Quota rent" represents the value that the license to export a certain amount of textiles or apparel to a restricted market of an industrial country confers on the quota holder. According to one set of estimates, quota rents generated by U.S. textile restraints alone were worth $3 billion in 1986. The total of quota rents for OECD nations is probably at least $10 billion. See Cline, *The Future of World Trade*, pp. 276-77.

24. Multinational enterprises tend to support freer trade, both because trade restrictions place a heavy burden on the substantial volume of transactions between their affiliates and because

trade restrictions impede the relocation of production facilities to countries that produce at lower cost.

25. The Textile Surveillance Body (TSB) meets under GATT auspices to monitor bilateral agreements for consistency with the principles of the Multifiber Agreement (MFA). The idea is to prevent overbearing behavior by powerful importers such as the European Community and the United States.

26. Tropical products are divided into seven classes: tropical beverages (mainly tea and coffee); spices, flowers, and plaiting products; certain oilseeds, vegetable oils, and tropical oilcakes; tobacco, rice, and tropical roots; fruits and nuts; natural rubber and tropical wood; and jute and hard fibers. The definitional and cross-referencing strategy enables "sensitive" products to be considered in the all-important negotiating group on agriculture; and that, in turn, has averted the creation of strong domestic lobbies in the industrial countries that might resist liberalization in trade of the remaining tropical products.

27. See GATT, *International Trade 1987/88,* vol. 1, appendix Table IV. The figure of $40 billion represents the sum of "oilseeds, fats, oils, oilcakes and meals" and "tropical beverages." The tropical products agreement reached in Montreal is said to have a trade coverage of $25-30 billion. See *Financial Times,* December 8, 1988, p. 5.

28. See *Inside U.S. Trade,* Special Report, September 30, 1988, and Special Report, December 7, 1988. The trade coverage of the U.S. offer is much lower than the European Community or the Japanese offer because almost all of the $16 billion of U.S. imports of tropical products have long entered the U.S. market on a duty-free basis. The United States successfully insisted that the developing countries make their own concessions on imported tropical products as a contribution to the group's work. See *Inside U.S. Trade,* November 11, 1988, p. 4, and December 16, 1988, p. 3; *Financial Times,* December 6, 1988, p. 1.

29. For general background, see Dale E. Hathaway, *Agriculture and the GATT: Rewriting the Rules* (Washington, D.C.: Institute for International Economics, September 1987); Robert L. Paarlberg, *Fixing Farm Trade: Policy Options for the United States* (Cambridge, Mass.: Council on Foreign Relations, Ballinger Publishing, 1988); Institute for International

Economics, *Reforming World Agricultural Trade*, Washington, D.C., May 1988; Carlisle Ford Runge, "Agricultural Protectionism," *Foreign Affairs*, Fall 1988; Vernon Roningen and Praveen Dixit, "Economic Implications of Agricultural Policy Reform in Industrial Market Economies," U.S. Department of Agriculture, Economic Research Service, May 1989.

30. See GATT, *International Trade 1987/88*, vol. 1, Table 19.

31. See Hathaway, *Agriculture and the GATT*, pp. 77, 87; *The New York Times*, December 11, 1988, p. E3. For additional cost estimates, see Organization for Economic Cooperation and Development, *National Priorities and Agricultural Trade*, Paris, 1987, pp. 50-53.

The European Community's Common Agricultural Policy (CAP) is particularly disruptive of world trade in agricultural products. The CAP consumes around 60 to 70 percent of the European Community budget. It has been designed to maintain farm incomes by keeping European agricultural prices high and insulating them from fluctuations in world prices. This goal has been achieved by variable tariffs on imports (the lower the world prices, the higher the tariff) and by export subsidies (to bridge the gap between high internal prices and world prices). These policies shift most of Western Europe's agricultural problems onto world markets, to the great annoyance of the United States and other agricultural exporting nations.

32. See World Bank, *World Bank Development Report 1986*, Washington, D.C., 1986, p. 129.

33. According to an estimate provided by Clayton Yeutter, protectionist measures cut developing countries' agricultural exports to industrial countries by approximately $27 billion. See *The New York Times*, December 10, 1988, p. 39. In addition, the trade of OECD countries is probably reduced by $60 to $80 billion annually.

34. One significant achievement of the Dillon Round (1960-61) was a European Community binding on the tariffs applied to oilseeds and oilseed products and certain nongrain animal feedstuffs (soybean meal, tapioca, corn gluten, citrus pulp). Ever since the 1960s, the European Community has tried to design farm support programs and implement trade policies that would effectively undercut the Dillon Round tariff bindings. Such Euro-

pean Community efforts invariably prompt vociferous protests from the United States and other exporters. See Hathaway, *Agriculture and the GATT,* pp. 74-75.

35. Led by Australian Prime Minister Robert Hawke, the Cairns Group includes four industrial countries (Australia, Canada, Hungary, and New Zealand) and ten developing countries (Argentina, Brazil, Chile, Colombia, Fiji, Indonesia, Malaysia, the Philippines, Thailand, and Uruguay). The Australian minister for trade, Michael Duffy, and the Australian ambassador to the GATT, Alan Oxley, deserve much of the credit for sparking the Cairns Group and keeping pressure on Western Europe and the United States in the Uruguay Round talks. See *Financial Times,* December 7, 1988, p. 7.

36. It will not be easy for the Bush administration to sell these ideas on farm trade to Congress when the basic U.S. farm legislation, the Food Security Act of 1985, comes up for renewal in 1990. The chairman of the Senate Agricultural Committee, Senator Patrick Leahy (D-Vt.) said, "We're not going to junk our present programs unless we've got a better alternative" (see *Journal of Commerce,* February 10, 1987, p. 12A). Senator David Karnes (R-Neb.) killed his own reelection bid by proclaiming, "We need fewer farmers" and proposing the elimination of agricultural subsidies (see *The Washington Post,* October 23, 1988, p. A24). His fate will not be forgotten by other legislators from farm states, Democrat or Republican. On the other hand, Clayton Yeutter, the secretary of agriculture, is a dedicated and persuasive opponent of farm subsidies. If anyone can push a deal through Congress, it is Yeutter.

37. See *Inside U.S. Trade,* "Special Report," July 18, 1988.

38. See *Inside U.S. Trade,* October 28, 1988, pp. 1, 7-8, 13-15, and November 11, 1988, p. 1; *The Wall Street Journal,* October 20, 1988, p. A21; *The New York Times,* November 18, 1988, p. D1.

39. See the submission by the European Community, "An Approach for a Concerted Reduction in the Long Term," Geneva, October 14, 1988, reproduced in *Inside U.S. Trade,* October 21, 1988.

40. To be sure, the European Community has recently taken small steps in the direction of reform. For example, a production-control program for milk, introduced in 1984, was tightened in

1987, and in February 1988 the Council of Ministers adopted automatic price cuts once specific farm quotas are exceeded. But the United States remains skeptical. According to a cabinet paper prepared before the Montreal meeting:

> The major obstacle continues to be the policy intransigence of the European Community. In March, the EC Council of Ministers took a number of steps which were portrayed as improvements of the situation in agricultural world markets. Unfortunately, we have concluded that although the EC actions may have been politically difficult and may have solved the Community's immediate budgetary problems, they clearly failed to deal adequately with the root cause of world agriculture problems: government supports linked to production. Furthermore, we believe that the measures will result in increased trade distortions working against our interests, rather than setting EC policy on a course toward a comprehensive, market-oriented approach to reforms. (See *Inside U.S. Trade,* "Special Report," September 30, 1988).

To such accusations, the European Community trade commissioner, Willy de Clercq, replied: "The American proposal is nothing more than an effort to dismantle CAP. And those who seek to dismantle the CAP will find that we will not permit this to happen." See *The Wall Street Journal,* December 12, 1988, p. A4.

In rhetorical terms, the United States, the European Community, and the Cairns Group came much closer to agreement in the April 1989 meeting held in Geneva. See *The New York Times,* April 8, 1989, p. 33; *Europe-1992,* April 12, 1989, p. 103; *The Economist,* April 15, 1989, p. 13.

In October 1989, the United States proposed that production subsidies be substantially reduced over ten years, and that export subsidies be phased out over five years. The European Community voiced its strong objections. See *Journal of Commerce,* October 29, 1989, p. 10A.

41. Japan has proposed indefinite protection of selected commodities for food security reasons (this formulation was tailored to protect Japanese rice farmers) but otherwise has called for

liberalization. Japan kept a low profile in Montreal while sympathizing with the European Community go-slow approach.

42. Between 1980 and 1985, the United States initiated 23 "regular" safeguard actions, the European Community initiated 7, Australia initiated 4, and Canada initiated 4. Many of these "regular" actions did not result in safeguard measures. See J. Michael Finger and Julio Nogues, "International Control of Subsidies and Countervailing Duties," *The World Bank Economic Review*, September 1987, Table 1. However, there are now more than 250 "voluntary" restraint agreements in effect, operating to limit imports outside the disciplines of Article 19. Some 200 of these have been initiated by the European Community and the United States. See *The New York Times*, June 28, 1989, p. D2.

43. The June 1989 Draft Text by the chairman of the Negotiating Group on Safeguards, together with a submission from the European Community, are reproduced in *Inside U.S. Trade*, "Special Report," June 30, 1989. The United States and the European Community both advocate selectivity.

44. The six major codes negotiated in the Tokyo Round are Government Procurement, Customs Valuation, Technical Barriers to Trade (Standards), Import Licensing Procedures, Antidumping, and Subsidies and Countervailing Measures. For a brief summary, see Gilbert R. Winham, *International Trade and the Tokyo Round Negotiations* (Princeton, N.J.: Princeton University Press, 1986).

45. See Finger and Nogues, "International Control of Subsidies and Countervailing Duties," Table 1. The overall score for 1980–88 is: United States, 420 cases initiated (and 167 antidumping duties now in place); European Community, 330 cases initiated. See *The Economist*, December 3, 1988, p. 15.

46. This warning has been sounded by Brian Hindley of the Trade Policy Research Centre in London and Patrick Messerlin of the World Bank in Washington, D.C. One reason for concern reflects the fact that antidumping statutes generally contain a cost standard that requires import prices to equal or exceed the fully allocated average costs of production (including a "proper" allocation for sunk capital costs and research and development costs). Quite often, in the normal conduct of

business, firms simply do not (and cannot) price their products to recoup sunk costs. Yet, under the antidumping law, they are guilty of "unfair" trade. For a legal analysis, see Judith Hippler Bello and Alan F. Holmer, *The Antidumping and Countervailing Duty Laws* (Chicago: American Bar Association, 1987).

47. Jeffrey Schott at the Institute for International Economics in Washington, D.C., is undertaking a study on coordination among GATT, the International Monetary Fund, and the World Bank.

48. There have been prolonged and unsatisfactory conclusions to any number of agricultural disputes. As one terrible example, the U.S. complaint about European pasta subsidies took twelve years to resolve, and even then the European Community refused to accept an adverse panel report. See *Inside U.S. Trade,* October 21, 1988, pp. 3-4.

49. For several years the United States has been prepared to take retaliatory Section 301 action based on a favorable panel finding, irrespective of whether the Council of Ministers has adopted the panel report. Therefore, the practical consequence of retaining the power of the parties to block the adoption of panel reports is limited, at least for the United States. Nevertheless, discussion continues on the consensus minus two proposal. One possibility, floated by the European Community, is to permit remedial action to be taken on a "consensus minus two" basis (the existing U.S. practice), but to insist that panel findings not be incorporated into the body of GATT law until consensus acceptance by the Council of Ministers.

50. For example, when Nicaragua obtained a GATT ruling that U.S. sanctions against Nicaraguan exports were not consistent with the national security provisions of GATT Article 21, the United States simply ignored the ruling, and Nicaragua had no effective recourse.

51. In the United States software is protected by copyright laws, while semiconductor masks (basic design templates) are protected by the Semiconductor Chip Protection Act of 1986. The United States seeks equivalent protection in other countries. By contrast, trade secrets are not registered and remain protected only as long as the holder keeps them from slipping into the domain of common knowledge. Trade secrecy laws dif-

fer from country to country (and even within the United States), and this subject probably will not be covered by the Trade-Related Intellectual Property Rights Group.

See, generally, Helena Stalson, *Intellectual Property Rights and U.S. Competitiveness in Trade* (Washington, D.C.: National Planning Association, 1987); Robert P. Benko, *Protecting Intellectual Rights: Issues and Controversies* (Washington, D.C.: American Enterprise Institute, 1987); and C. Michael Hathaway, "Negotiations on Trade Related Property Rights in the Uruguay Round," in Practising Law Institute, *Trade Law and Policy Institute,* Course Handbook no. 510, Washington, D.C., September 1989.

52. See U.S. International Trade Commission, *Foreign Protection of Intellectual Property Rights and the Effect on U.S. Industry and Trade,* Washington, D.C., February 1988. For a review of the estimates of piracy, see Steven Globerman Associates Ltd., "The Economic Consequences of Product Piracy," Report to the National Chamber Foundation, Washington, D.C., September 1988.

53. See *Financial Times,* September 14, 1988, p. 7. If accurate, this estimate suggests that counterfeit goods entering international trade amount to $75-150 billion annually.

54. Within the United States, holders of intellectual property rights can protect their markets against pirated or counterfeit imports by invoking Section 337 procedures before the U.S. International Trade Commission.

55. See *Inside U.S. Trade,* Special Report, July 22, 1988; *Inside U.S. Trade,* July 7, 1989, pp. 10-13.

56. See *Inside U.S. Trade,* December 2, 1988, pp. 3-4.

57. See *Journal of Commerce,* December 6, 1988, p. 1. Also see *Financial Times,* June 27, 1989, p. 6.

58. In December 1988 a GATT panel found against the U.S. application of Section 337 on the grounds that the statute denies importers the same recourse to U.S. courts that is enjoyed by domestic defendants in patent, copyright, and trademark infringement actions. The United States has said that it will amend Section 337 only in the context of a satisfactory outcome to the TRIPs negotiation. See *Inside U.S. Trade,* July 7, 1989, p. 5.

59. For a running account of Thailand's response to U.S. pressure, see *Inside U.S. Trade,* November 4, 1988, p. 1; *Jour-*

nal of Commerce, December 13, 1988, p. 5A; *The Wall Street Journal,* December 23, 1988, p. A4. By November 1989, South Korea, Taiwan, and Saudi Arabia had initiated crackdowns against pirated versions of U.S. films, records, pharmaceuticals, software, and other products; and the United States eased its threat of trade sanctions against those three countries. See *The New York Times,* November 2, 1989, p. D1.

60. For a discussion of the trade-related investment issues as they apply to developing countries, see Theodore H. Moran, ed., *Investing in Development: New Roles for Private Capital* (Washington, D.C.: Overseas Development Council, 1986); and Theodore H. Moran and Charles Pearson, "Tread Carefully in the Field of TRIP Measures," *The World Economy,* March 1988. For a review of events in OECD nations, see Donald L. Guertin and John M. Kline, "Building an International Investment Accord" (unpublished manuscript, Georgetown University, Washington, D.C., October 28, 1988).

61. See Gary Hufbauer, *Tax Treaties and American Interests,* Report to the National Foreign Trade Council, New York, 1988, Table 3.

62. See Gerald West, "Issues in Global Management," *Directors and Boards,* Fall 1988, p. 27.

63. In October 1988 the Senate gave its consent to the ratification of bilateral investment treaties with eight countries: Bangladesh, Cameroon, Egypt, Grenada, Morocco, Senegal, Turkey, and Zaire. For foreign policy reasons, treaties signed with Panama and Haiti were not ratified. In the world at large, 308 BITs have been negotiated by 16 industrial countries, 86 developing countries, and 48 Communist countries. See Peter Peters, "Investment Treaties: An Updating," Report to the International Law Association, Warsaw Conference 1988, July 1, 1988.

64. For a systematic analysis of trade in services, see Geza Feketekuty, *International Trade in Services: An Overview and Blueprint for Negotiations* (Cambridge, Mass.: American Enterprise Institute, Ballinger Publishing, 1988). Also see Jacques J. Reinstein, *The Uruguay Round of Multilateral Trade Negotiation under GATT: Policy Proposals on Trade and Services* (Washington, D.C.: Atlantic Council, 1987); Helena Stalson,

U.S. Service Exports and Foreign Business (Washington, D.C.:
National Planning Association, 1985); Jagdish N. Bhagwati,
"Trade in Services and the Multilateral Trade Negotiations,"
World Bank Economic Review, September 1987; Overseas
Development Council, "Negotiating U.S.–Third World Trade
in Services: Obstacles and Opportunities," Washington, D.C.,
1986; Irving Kravis and Robert Lipsey, "Production and Trade
in Services by U.S. Multinational Firms," NBER Working Paper
2615, October 1988. For an update on the GATT talks, see *Financial Times,* May 22, 1989, p. 18; *Inside U.S. Trade,* April 21, 1989,
p. 7; and *Journal of Commerce,* May 3, 1989, p. 1A. For recent
data, see GATT, *International Trade 1988/89,* vol. 1, chapter 3;
and OECD, *OECD Member Countries' Data on Trade in Services,* Paris, 1987.

65. The head of the Indian delegation to the GATT talks was
quoted as saying: "If a country wants to bring its own people
to run a bank in our country, we would like to take our people
to run hotels in their countries." See *Journal of Commerce,*
December 8, 1988, p. 1.

66. Isaiah Frank of the Johns Hopkins School for Advanced
International Studies has been a notable exponent of the code
approach.

67. Both problems were evident in the negotiations that led
to the Tokyo Round Code on Subsidies and Countervailing
Measures. See Gary Clyde Hufbauer and Joanna Shelton Erb,
Subsidies in International Trade (Washington, D.C.: Institute
for International Economics, 1984).

68. Former U.S. Trade Representative Clayton Yeutter has
complained: "[The EC] told me they can't be negotiating inter-
nally on the new rules and negotiate with us at the same time."
See *The Wall Street Journal,* August 1, 1988, p. 1. But delay-
ing the Uruguay Round will not appreciably improve the quality
of European Community participation.

Chapter 4

1. For a more enthusiastic view of sector arrangements, see
Clyde Prestowitz, "Set Guidelines for Export Market Share,"
The New York Times, December 11, 1988, p. F2.

2. The sequence of textile and apparel arrangements and their

implications for consumers and producers are summarized by Gary Clyde Hufbauer, Diane T. Berliner, and Kimberly Ann Elliott, *Trade Protection in the United States: 31 Case Studies* (Washington, D.C.: Institute for International Economics, 1986), pp. 117-53; World Bank, *World Development Report 1987,* Washington, D.C., 1987, pp. 136-37. For an in-depth study, see William R. Cline, *The Future of World Trade in Textiles and Apparel* (Washington, D.C.: Institute for International Economics, 1987).

3. As an additional concession to U.S. industry, most textiles and apparel were exempted from tariff cuts in the Kennedy Round.

4. See Hufbauer, Berliner, and Elliott, *Trade Protection in the United States,* p. 141.

5. See *The New York Times,* September 24, 1988, p. 1.

6. See *Journal of Commerce,* September 26, 1988, pp. 1A-2A.

7. See Vincent Cable, "Textiles and Clothing in a New Round of Trade Negotiations," *The World Bank Economic Review,* Washington, D.C., September 1987.

8. For possible exit paths from the Multifiber Agreement morass, see Gary Clyde Hufbauer and Howard F. Rosen, *Trade Policy for Troubled Industries* (Washington, D.C.: Institute for International Economics, 1986), chap. 5; Gary Clyde Hufbauer and Jeffrey J. Schott, *Trading for Growth: The Next Round of Trade Negotiations* (Washington, D.C.: Institute for International Economics, 1985), pp. 33-61; and Martin Wolf, "How to Unravel the Multi-Fibre Arrangement," *The World Economy,* September 1985. In the fall of 1989, U.S. Trade Representative Carla Hills began quietly exploring avenues to phase out the MFA.

Note, however, that the House textile caucus is already planning tactics for derailing any liberalization of the MFA in the Uruguay Round. See *Inside U.S. Trade,* April 14, 1989, p. 4.

9. This account draws heavily on Clyde V. Prestowitz, Jr., *Trading Places: How We Allowed Japan to Take the Lead* (New York: Basic Books, 1988), chap. 2; and Thomas R. Howell et al., *The Microelectronics Race* (Boulder, Colo.: Westview Press, 1988). Also see Semiconductor Industry Association, "Two Years of Experience under the U.S.-Japan Semiconductor Agreement," Cupertino, Calif., September 1988; Electronics Industries

Association of Japan, "Statement on Semiconductors," Washington, D.C., November 21, 1988.

10. Dynamic random access memory chips serve as memory banks for many electronic products. The first DRAM was able to store about 1,000 bits (1K) of information. For technical reasons, DRAM capacities increase by multiples of four.

11. The microprocessor is a single integrated circuit chip that performs the central processing functions of a computer.

12. The Japanese strategy is based on producing very large volumes, and experience showed that a doubling of volume enabled a reduction of unit costs by 20 to 30 percent. In addition, the successful production of one generation of chips (for example, the 64K DRAM) provided a head start in research and development on the next generation (for example, the 256K DRAM).

13. Between September 1984 and September 1985, the price of 64K DRAMs (then the industry standard) imported from Japan dropped from $3.50 to $1.00. See Howell et al., *The Microelectronics Race,* p. 87.

14. Japanese firms had, in fact, captured 90 percent of the world market for 256K DRAMs. See *Science,* November 22, 1985, p. 918. The worldwide electronics industry now depends on a few large Japanese companies, such as Hitachi, Toshiba, NEC, Mitsubishi, and Fujitsu, for about 80 percent of its standardized memory chips. See *The New York Times,* August 2, 1988.

15. The EPROM is an erasable, programmable read-only memory chip that is blank at manufacture, which enables the user to install customized programs at a later date. The EPROM allows great flexibility because a program can be erased from it and replaced by a new one.

As recently as February 1989, U.S. companies announced the development of a new one-million-transistor microprocessor that combines graphics and number-crunching components in a single chip. The new chips are examples of more powerful microprocessors based on a design approach known as reduced instruction set computing (RISC). They represent another significant departure from the standardized memory chip market.

16. See Judith Hippler Bello and Alan F. Holmer, "Section 301 of the Trade Act of 1984: Requirements, Procedures, and Developments," *Northwestern Journal of International Law and Business,* Fall-Winter 1986. The agreement contained provisions other than those relating to market access and dumping. For example, both governments agreed to make sure that foreign companies would obtain full access to patents that result from government-sponsored research and development.

17. See *The Wall Street Journal,* February 12, 1987, p. 1; July 18, 1988, p. 2.

18. See *The New York Times,* November 19, 1988, p. 33.

19. See *Inside U.S. Trade,* September 23, 1988, p. 4, November 18, 1988, p. 1, and June 9, 1989, p. 17; *The New York Times,* November 19, 1988, p. 33.

20. All in all, the Second Semiconductor Agreement has harmed the U.S. computer industry. When demand for DRAMs increased enormously in mid-1987, U.S. producers could not keep up. The shortage of DRAMS forced U.S. computer makers to curtail production and delay new models. When gluts arise in the world memory chip market or when certain chips are scarce, U.S. computer firms find that their vertically integrated Japanese competitors have better access to low-cost or scarce chips. See "How the Computer Companies Lost Their Memories," *Forbes,* June 13, 1988; *Financial Times,* September 16, 1988, p. 1.

21. To fight against such practices, the European Community lodged a complaint in GATT in October 1986, prevailed in the GATT panel proceedings in mid-1987, and in May 1988 persuaded the GATT Council to adopt the panel report. More important, the European Community initiated its own $4 billion government-subsidized project (JESSI) to develop up-to-date technology. The two main beneficiaries of this project are Siemens AG and Philips, N.V. It is not that the European Community objects in principle to managed trade; the critical point is that the European Community wants European trade to be managed from Brussels, not Tokyo or Washington. In fact, the European Community has now negotiated its own semiconductor agreement with Japan.

22. See Howell et al., *The Microelectronics Race,* p. 41.

THE FREE TRADE DEBATE

23. The chief executive officer of Semiconductor Manufacturing Technology (Sematech) is Robert N. Noyce, a cofounder (in 1957) of Fairchild Semiconductor, the vice-chairman of Intel, and a respected patriarch of Silicon Valley. See *Business Week,* August 15, 1988, pp. 76-79. U.S. Memories will led by Sanford Kane, a former vice president of IBM. IBM will also license its 4-megabit DRAM chip design to the new joint venture. See *Financial Times,* June 23, 1989, p. 25, and *Inside U.S. Trade,* June 30, 1989, p. 3.

Equally important in the long-run survival strategy of U.S. firms will be joint-venture arrangements with Japanese producers, as exemplified by the Texas Instruments-Hitachi announcement of a joint project to develop a 16-megabit DRAM. See *The Washington Post,* December 23, 1988, p. D1. Similar joint ventures are an important component of the revival of the U.S. automobile and steel industries.

The National Cooperation Research Act of 1984 provides an antitrust exemption for research and development joint ventures. Legislation to provide a similar exemption for manufacturing joint ventures has been introduced by Representative Tom Campbell (R-Calif.) and Representative Don Edwards (D-Calif.). See *Inside U.S. Trade,* June 9, 1989, p. 3.

24. See *Financial Times,* September 16, 1988, p. 1; September 27, 1988, p. 28.

25. This conclusion draws heavily on David D. Hale, "The Post Chicago Era in American Economic Policy," *The Marcus Wallenberg Papers on International Finance* 2, no. 3 (International Law Institute, 1989).

26. The standard arguments against the likelihood of a successful industrial policy are: (1) it is difficult to pick winners; (2) the United States does not have an elite civil service comparable to that employed in Japan and other industrial countries (the U.S. president makes more than 3,000 political appointments to the executive branch, compared to 0 for the Japanese prime minister, 60 for the West German chancellor, and about 150 for the British prime minister); (3) industrial policy is usually captured by the most powerful lobby of the day, which often represents the industry of yesterday rather than the industry of tomorrow.

27. When the government wishes to stimulate an industry, it can provide an on-budget subsidy—money from the public treasury—or it can provide an off-budget subsidy—such as protection from foreign competition. Sector trade arrangements usually involve huge, out-of-sight, off-budget subsidies to protected industries.

28. The Omnibus Trade and Competitiveness Act of 1988, in fact, specifically promotes the bilateral negotiation of level playing fields in telecommunications (through the mechanism of the U.S. trade representative designation of "priority countries" for achieving better U.S. market access) and in certain financial services (through the primary dealer provisions that require equivalent access to markets for treasury bills and bonds). In addition, the 1988 act provides a general spur to the opening of foreign markets through the "Super 301" provisions, discussed in Chapter 5.

Chapter 5

1. See Asher Isaacs, *International Trade: Tariff and Commercial Policies* (Chicago: Richard D. Irwin, 1948), chaps. 13, 17.

2. See John H. Jackson and William J. Davey, *International Economic Relations* (St. Paul: West Publishing Co., 1986), pp. 355-56, 407-8. Ironically, the U.S. tariffs imposed on light trucks subsequently served to protect Volkswagen production in the United States against Japanese competition.

3. See ibid., pp. 664, 727, 799.

4. In addition to the commonplace use of retaliation to address unfair imports and export barriers, there is growing congressional interest in designing retaliatory tools to address workers' rights (provisions appear in the Trade Act of 1974, the Trade and Tariff Act of 1984, the Trade and International Economic Policy Reform Act of 1986, and the Omnibus Trade and Competitiveness Act of 1988) and to protect endangered wildlife (starting with the Fisherman's Protection Act of 1967 and extending to the proposals offered by Senator Daniel Patrick Moynihan (D-N.Y.) in 1988 to invoke Section 301 for this purpose).

5. For a tally of actions between 1974 and 1985, see Jackson and Davey, *International Economic Relations,* p. 809. Section

301 is based on antecedents in the Trade Expansion Act of 1962. For an account of actions between 1986 and 1988, see Earl Grinols, "Procedural Protectionism: The American Trade Bill and the New Interventionist Mode," Council of Economic Advisers, Washington, D.C., 1988; and *Inside U.S. Trade,* February 3, 1989, p. 8. The active caseload of Section 301 cases almost doubled between the period 1975-81 (an average of eight cases) and the period 1982-88 (an average of sixteen cases).

6. For an account of the May 1989 Super 301 initiatives, see *Inside U.S. Trade,* May 26, 1989, p. 1; *Journal of Commerce,* May 30, 1989, p. 1A; and *Financial Times,* June 21, 1989, p. 7. For an overview, see A. Jane Bradley, "The 'Super 301' Process," in Practising Law Institute, *Trade Law and Policy Institute,* Course Handbook no. 510, Washington, D.C., September 1989.

7. See William R. Cline, *Reciprocity: A New Approach to World Trade Policy?* (Washington, D.C.: Institute for International Economics, September 1982), pp. 21-30; Klaus Stegemann, "Antidumping Policy and the Consumer," *Journal of World Trade Law,* September 1985; Alan F. Holmer, Statement of General Counsel, Office of United States Trade Representative, before the International Trade Subcommittee of the House Ways and Means Committee, April 15, 1986.

8. See Judith Hippler Bello and Alan F. Holmer, "Section 301 of the Trade Act of 1984: Requirements, Procedures, and Developments," *Northwestern Journal of International Law and Business,* Fall-Winter 1986. The figure of $1 billion is based on average U.S. exports in the period 1981-83.

9. See *Journal of Commerce,* October 21, 1988, p. 1; *Inside U.S. Trade,* October 28, 1988, p. 1. The trade coverage of sanctioned products was only $39 million, less than one-half of 1 percent of U.S. imports from Brazil.

10. See *Journal of Commerce,* October 14, 1988, p. 6A; *The Wall Street Journal,* June 1, 1989, p. A6.

11. See *Financial Times,* October 7, 1988, p. 1.

12. See *Financial Times,* August 3, 1988, p. 14.

13. See *Inside U.S. Trade,* December 2, 1988, p. 1, and subsequent issues for a running account of this episode.

Chapter 6

1. In this chapter the term "free trade area" is used broadly to include customs unions. In a customs union (or common market), all members impose a common external tariff; in a free trade area (narrowly defined), each member retains its own external tariff.

2. See Jacob Viner, *The Customs Union Issue* (New York: Carnegie Endowment for International Peace, 1950). For an update and current appraisal, see Jeffrey J. Schott, ed., *More Free Trade Areas?* (Washington, D.C.: Institute for International Economics, 1989).

3. When the free trade area covers a broader range of products, the diversionary outcome becomes less likely. Moreover, a true free trade area is less likely to divert trade than a customs union because the common tariff of a customs union will very likely entail higher tariffs for some countries or some products, by comparison with the tariffs applied by the individual countries prior to the customs union. See Paul Wonnacott and Mark Lutz, "More Free Trade Associations?" in Schott, ed., *More Free Trade Areas?*

4. The original six signatories of the Treaty of Rome were Belgium, the Federal Republic of Germany, France, Italy, Luxembourg, and the Netherlands; in 1973, they were joined by Denmark, Ireland, and the United Kingdom; in 1981, by Greece; in 1986, by Portugal and Spain. (The Norwegian government agreed to join in 1973 but declined after accession was rejected in a national referendum.)

5. See *Completing the Internal Market,* White Paper from the Commission to the European Council, Brussels, 1985. The discussion that follows draws on Michael Calingaert, *The 1992 Challenge from Europe: Development of the European Community's Internal Market* (Washington, D.C.: National Planning Assocation, 1988); Paolo Cecchini, *The European Challenge, 1992: The Benefits of a Single Market* (Hants, England: Wildwood House Ltd., 1988); Morgan Guaranty Trust Company, *World Financial Markets,* September 1988; Carl B. Hamilton, *The New Protectionism and International Economic Integration,* European Free Trade Association, Occasional Paper no. 21, Geneva, 1987.

6. See Calingaert, *The 1992 Challenge from Europe,* p. 33.

7. See *Financial Times,* October 18, 1988, p. 2. It is worth noting a most important procedural device known as the mutual recognition approach: Rather than adopt a single European standard for every good and service (dishwashers, automobiles, life insurance), the presumption is that, if the good or service is acceptable in the home market of the producing country, it will be acceptable throughout the European Community. Only for a limited range of goods and services will common European Community standards be devised.

8. See Cecchini, *The European Challenge, 1992.* In contrast to Cecchini's findings, a study conducted in 1987 by Data Resources, Inc., projects a gain of only 0.5 percent in GDP by 1992 and only 300,000 additional jobs by 1995. Data Resources, Inc., *The European Internal Market,* Brussels, 1987, Executive Summary.

9. See *Financial Times,* August 31, 1988, p. 4

10. See M. Peter McPherson, "The European Community's Internal Market Program: An American Perspective," *Treasury News,* Department of the Treasury, August 4, 1988. A parallel to the current mixture of U.S. admiration and concern can be found in the late 1950s and early 1960s when the United States initially championed the formation of the Common Market as a political counterweight to Eastern Europe but later grew nervous about its commercial ramifications.

11. "We have not successfully rolled back the frontiers of the state in Britain only to see them reimposed at a European level." *Financial Times,* September 21, 1988, p. 1.

12. West German officials, for example, have announced that they do not support protectionist proposals such as the reciprocity requirement for banks, the expansion of existing French and Italian quotas on foreign autos to the entire European Community, and the proposal on government procurement that would ask members to give preferences to products that are manufactured to the extent of 50 percent or more in the European Community. See Hans Tietmeyer, "1992, Ho!" *The International Economy,* September/October 1988, pp. 72-73; *Inside U. S. Trade,* September 23, 1988, p. 2; and *The Christian Science Monitor,* June 30, 1988, p. 10.

13. See Ingo Walter, *Global Competition in Financial Services: Market Structure, Protection and Trade Liberalization* (Cambridge, Mass.: Ballinger Publishing, 1988).

14. See Calingaert, *The 1992 Challenge from Europe,* p. 114.

15. See Jonathan David Aronson and Peter F. Cowhey, *When Countries Talk: International Trade in Telecommunications Services* (Cambridge, Mass.: Ballinger Publishing, 1988).

16. See Coudert Brothers, "Major Developments in U.S. Trade Law: Ten Sections of the Omnibus Trade and Competitiveness Act of 1988," Washington, D.C., 1988, pp. 9-12.

17. See *Towards a Dynamic European Economy,* Green Paper on the Development of the Common Market for Telecommunications Services and Equipment, Brussels, 1987. Historically the Western European market for telecommunications equipment has been severely fragmented by differing national standards and discriminatory procurement practices. Philips, N.V., for example, produces seven kinds of television sets equipped with different tuners, semiconductors, and plugs to meet differing Western European national standards. A staff of seventy engineers does nothing other than adjust new models to local requirements.

18. See U.S. Trade Representative, "Response of the Government of the United States of America to the European Community Green Paper on the Development of the Common Market for Telecommunications Services and Equipment," Washington, D.C., November/December 1987.

19. For detailed commentary on the Free Trade Agreement, see Peter Morici, "The Canada-U.S. Free Trade Agreement: Origins and Prospects" (paper presented at Lehigh University Conference on Economic Aspects of Regional Trading Arrangements, May 25-26, 1988, revised June 1988); Jeffrey J. Schott and Murray G. Smith, *The Canada-United States Free Trade Agreement: The Global Impact,* Institute for International Economics and Institute for Public Policy, Washington, D.C., and Ottawa, 1988; Gilbert R. Winham, *Trading with Canada: The Canada-U.S. Free Trade Agreement* (New York: Twentieth Century Fund, 1988); Robert M. Stern, Philip H. Trezise, and John Whalley, *Perspectives on a U.S.-Canadian Free Trade Agreement* (Washington, D.C.: Brookings Institution, 1987); William

Diebold, Jr., ed., *Bilateralism, Multilateralism and Canada in U.S. Trade Policies* (Cambridge, Mass.: Council on Foreign Relations, Ballinger Publishing, 1988).

20. From a short-term perspective, the 1988 Free Trade Agreement can be viewed as the outgrowth of the 1965 U.S.-Canada Automobile Agreement. The auto pact grew out of a contentious countervailing duty petition, and eventually led to an agreement that eliminated tariffs on all original autos and parts and provided investment safeguards for Canada. The auto pact gave a substantial push to the Canadian car industry. In 1961, Canada exported a mere 175 vehicles to the United States; in 1966, one year after the pact was concluded, car exports from Canada to the United States were almost 147,000; and by 1985 they reached more than 1 million.

21. Canadian ratification of the Free Trade Agreement amounted to a repeal of "Beigie's Law": when the economy is doing well, Canadians supposedly prefer more nationalism to closer economic ties with the United States. Carl Beigie is a prominent Canadian economist and a former director of the C. D. Howe Institute.

Post-ratification appraisals of the pact, widely judged a success, appear in *The Washington Post,* June 25, 1989, p. H1, and *Journal of Commerce,* June 28, 1989, p. 1A.

22. Often discussed (and even contemplated by candidate Reagan in his call for a North American Accord in the 1980 presidential election) has been a deal with Mexico. But Mexican fears over sovereignty and identity are far stronger than Canadian concerns, and a broad trade agreement seems a more distant prospect. See *The New York Times,* November 24, 1988, p. D1. Bilateral talks designed to promote liberal sector arrangements, however, are possible not only with Mexico but also with Japan and other Pacific nations. See *Journal of Commerce,* December 16, 1988, p. 8A; *Inside U.S. Trade,* April 14, 1989, and May 26, 1989. In October 1989, Commerce Secretary Robert Mosbacher called for a U.S.-Mexican free trade pact that would eventually be extended to all Latin America. See *Journal of Commerce,* October 19, 1989, p. 1A.

23. For details, see Winham, *Trading with Canada,* pp. 46-49. The acceleration of tariff cuts on many products was agreed in June 1989.

24. See Schott and Smith, *The Canada-United States Free Trade Agreement,* p. 17.

25. Ibid., p. 18. The Economic Council of Canada subsequently revised its estimate of the creation of Canadian jobs to 250,000.

26. Ibid., p. 6.

27. Ibid., chap. 5; Winham, *Trading with Canada,* pp. 62-64.

28. See *Financial Post,* March 9, 1987, p. 1.

29. The establishment of a joint commission and the provision for binding arbitration are novel to the Canada-U.S. FTA. Notification and consultation follow from existing GATT practices. The FTA dispute settlement procedures are not limited to countervailing duty and antidumping actions, but different dispute procedures are provided for other issues. Some of the early disputes to be addressed under FTA procedures involve plywood tariff reductions (the United States claims it need not reduce its tariffs until common standards are agreed); salmon and herring (Canada has banned the export of its Pacific catch, depriving U.S. processors of raw fish); and two U.S. Commerce Department antidumping rulings (involving red raspberries and road-paving replacement parts).

30. Protection was "justified" as a response to trade restrictions on agricultural products by other OECD nations. Under the government of Prime Minister David Lange, however, New Zealand has dramatically liberalized its protected economy. It pulled down a historically high tariff wall and began to eradicate an archaic import licensing process. Under Prime Minister Robert Hawke, Australia has embarked on a similar path of unilaterally reducing its external tariff and quota barriers.

31. For detailed information about the Australia-New Zealand CER, see Australian Department of Foreign Affairs, *Australia-New Zealand Closer Economic Relations Trade Agreement: Documents Arising from 1988 Review,* Canberra, 1988; and Australian Department of Trade, *CER Future Progress,* Canberra, 1985.

Chapter 7

1. The idea for an OECD free trade area dates back to a study group chaired by John Leddy for the Atlantic Council. See Atlantic Council, *GATT Plus: A Proposal for Trade Reform,* Washington, D.C., 1974.

2. It is important not to have long breaks between major international trade negotiations. The period between the conclusion of the Tokyo Round in 1979 and the initiation of the Uruguay Round in 1986 was a period of marked retrogression in trade policy.

3. See Senator Bill Bradley, Speech to the New York Economic Club, December 8, 1988. For Secretary Baker's latest Pacific Rim proposal, see *Financial Times,* June 29, 1989, p. 16.

Index